BLOWING WHISTLES

BLOWING WHISTLES

by Matthew Todd

JOSEF WEINBERGER PLAYS

LONDON

For my family who make me feel really proud –
Mum and Dad (bonus points for not passing out
during this), Steve and Adam. And for Alex, Simon
and Dave who may as well be family. And for
Charlotte and Rod. All with love and thanks.

BLOWING WHISTLES was produced at the Warehouse Theatre, Croydon on 27th May 2005. It was directed by Phil Willmott, the set designed by Martin Thomas and lighting designed by Hansjorg Schmidt. The cast was as follows:

JAMIE	Neil Henry
NIGEL	Joe Fredericks
MARK	Peter McNicholl

BLOWING WHISTLES was originally produced as a workshop production by Trilby Productions as part of Hearts, Heaven and Hard Words at the Jermyn Street Theatre, London on 8th July 2003. It was directed by Stephen Henry with the following cast:

JAMIE	Ian Bass
NIGEL	Patrick Ross
MARK	Tom Sawyer

Author's note:

BLOWING WHISTLES contains many specific cultural references. Producers are asked to contact the author with reference to updating them or making them territory-specific.

ACT ONE

While the audience enter the auditorium there should be pop love songs playing. This is broken by the electronic sound of a modem connecting a PC to the Internet, loudly to the point of distortion as the lights fade to black.

Gaybar by Electric Six plays.

Scene One

Interior of Nigel *and* Jamie's *flat. Friday night. Around 11pm. The flat and mood is light and bright. There are cards on a table, bottles and wrapping paper and several boxed presents.*

Jamie is listening to music on his headphones. Nigel *is sat at the computer.* Nigel *gets up.*

NIGEL   Jamie. (*Pause.*) Jamie!

             (Jamie *removes his headphones and as he does the music cuts.*)

JAMIE   What?

NIGEL   Now.

JAMIE   Now?

NIGEL   Yes. Ten or fifteen minutes maybe.

JAMIE   Oh. God, no. Who?

NIGEL   Just some guy . . . and this place is a mess.

JAMIE   He's not coming round to see an Ikea show home, is he?

NIGEL   (*to presents and wrapping*) There's shit everywhere. He'll think we live in some kind of gay slum.

JAMIE   I don't care what he thinks.

NIGEL   You will do when he comes in and we look like a pair of queenie pigs, won't you. (JAMIE *stares at him.* NIGEL *places more rubbish in the bin.*) Can we put this somewhere. That look's butch, doesn't it. Here's my ice-cream maker', bread maker and a lovely set of spatulas. He wants hot sex, not a tour round the Croydon branch of the WI. Once he's put his knickers back on we can all start baking for Harvest festival. Whoopee!

JAMIE   They're the butchest things in this flat.

NIGEL   I'm straight acting, thank you.

    (*He walks out to the kitchen.*)

JAMIE   You ain't gonna win the Oscar.

NIGEL   I heard that.

    (*He re-enters.*)

JAMIE   You are supposed to be focusing all your attention on me this weekend . . .

NIGEL   Yes I have done and I will do – tomorrow – but – first, we've got tonight. It's going to be fantastic. Should I put some booze out?

JAMIE   Well I need a drink.

NIGEL   Champagne?

JAMIE   No, I've been saving that. It's expensive and for tomorrow. Too expensive to waste on some cheap Gaydar whore. Why don't you give him some water? The cat's bowl's over there. (NIGEL *glares.*) There's some Breezers in the Fridge.

NIGEL   We need to get the mood right for when he gets here. Maybe we should have some hot gay porn on?

JAMIE   If you want . . .

NIGEL   What have we got? *Doctor Anal . . . Latino Spunk Gobblers . . .* or *Footballer's Wives*, series one?

JAMIE   No, don't. I feel we've got something unrealistic to live up to then.

          (NIGEL *looks at the cards.*)

NIGEL   Do something with them then, will you.

JAMIE   Nigel.

NIGEL   Go on.

JAMIE   What do you mean 'do something with them'?

NIGEL   It's not very sexy, having your anniversary cards all over the place, is it?

          (NIGEL *exits to the kitchen.*)

JAMIE   I'm not moving them. (*Beat.*) Jesus! (*He put the cards in a drawer.*) That really pisses me off.

          (*He pauses on the framed picture of them when they met. Beat. He puts it into a drawer.* NIGEL *enters with two Bacardi Breezers.*)

          This is hardly the time to be doing this but no, the winkle fairy is dancing on your shoulder and he must be obeyed. I'm tired, he's bound to be a beast, we've got to be up early tomorrow for Mardi Gras.

NIGEL   It's called Gay Pride again this year.

JAMIE   Oh, right. Novel. They've made up their minds,
         have they? Whatever, I don't want this person
         staying. (*Pause.*) Is that OK?

         (NIGEL *kisses him.*)

NIGEL   Yes. Did you enjoy tonight?

JAMIE   Yes, I did. Very nice to see everybody together.

NIGEL   Yes. Fun. Straight friends, family, presentable
         gays all together on one night, see slutty gays
         tomorrow. Everyone was well fed and watered.
         Music was good, people seemed happy. Your
         brother looked quite pleased showing off his gay
         brother and brother-in-law.

JAMIE   She was quite nice.

NIGEL   Yeah . . . ish. I don't like a tattoo on a woman. I
         preferred the last one.

JAMIE   I though she was nice and it all felt very modern.
         Cheers.

         (*He raises his Bacardi Breezer.*)

NIGEL   It's not twelve o'clock yet.

JAMIE   So what.

NIGEL   Cheers.

JAMIE   To us.

         (*They clink Breezer bottles.*)

NIGEL   Ten . . .

JAMIE   Thousand.

NIGEL   . . . very long, and . . . (JAMIE *frowns.*) . . . happy
         years.

(*They kiss.*)

JAMIE   You're the dinosaur.

           (JAMIE *makes a dinosaur noise and they both start laughing and hug.* JAMIE *continues and* NIGEL *stops, staring into space.*)

JAMIE   What?

NIGEL   Just thinking, it might actually have been nice to have had my mum here tonight.

JAMIE   Yes.

NIGEL   It just seemed wrong that she wasn't there, you know?

JAMIE   You could always pick up the phone?

NIGEL   Out of the blue?

JAMIE   No time like the present. Important dates. Family reunions. I s'pose it is a bit 'Trisha', isn't it. 'My gay son I spurned forgives me and wants me back'.

NIGEL   And we've got a different edition to be in tonight.

JAMIE   What's that?

NIGEL   'I can't get enough of my gorgeous boyfriend having sex with other men, it turns me on too much'.

JAMIE   Where's this guy coming from then?

NIGEL   Sanderstead.

JAMIE   Well he's gonna be here in a minute, isn't he.

NIGEL   Yes. Clear this shit up.

JAMIE   Fuck off. Clear it up yourself. (*They resume tidying.*) And can you make sure you put that away. (JAMIE *motions to* NIGEL'S *new jacket.*) It's brand bloody new. I don't want him sitting on it.

NIGEL   Ahhh, isn't that nice. It must have cost you a fortune.

JAMIE   Yes it did. But you're worth it. (*He flutters his eyelashes and smiles.*) Anything for you darling.

NIGEL   I'll take you away somewhere nice.

JAMIE   No Rush. (*A pause as* JAMIE *continues tidying.*) You know, I'm just a little bit annoyed. I don't see why we had to get rid of everybody so you could give a BJ to some troll from Beckenham or wherever the fuck it is. (*Beat.*) I cannot believe that we kicked Laura out when she's still depressed.

NIGEL   She's in a cab, she'll be fine. I still don't know why he doesn't leave her.

JAMIE   What are you talking about? What kind of bloke forgets his girlfriend's birthday? She thought he was going to surprise her any minute.

NIGEL   They need to spice things up a bit. That's the problem with straight people. Too sex-phobic. He should have taken her to a swinger's club.

JAMIE   I don't think being spit-roasted over a wine bar in Waddon was exactly what she had in mind.

NIGEL   She's not exactly Kate Moss, is she, you'd think she'd jump at the chance. She'd love it. She's the kind of girl who was invented for 'dogging'.

JAMIE   Don't be so nasty. She's my friend.

NIGEL   Got a good taste in presents, I'll give her that.

JAMIE   (*referring to state of flat*) Is this up to your requirements?

NIGEL   It'll do.

JAMIE   Have you got any pictures of this person?

NIGEL   Have a look at his profile. Looks gorgeous.

                 (*They go to the computer screen. Jamie has a bowl of leftover snacks. He grabs a breadstick.*)

JAMIE   Christ.

NIGEL   Hold on a minute.

JAMIE   Is that him?

NIGEL   No, that's Fuck-Me-Hard, up the Purley Way.

JAMIE   Did we meet him?

NIGEL   No, he's on holiday until August.

JAMIE   What does it say?

NIGEL   Real pigboy. Big time into cottaging, cruising, saunas, heavily into scat . . . and going to the park and going to Rudeboyz and general backrooms. (*Beat.*) Looking for a serious relationship.

JAMIE   I don't want to meet him, please. (JAMIE *clicks onto another profile.*) Oh, he's nice. I recognise him. (*He crunches on his breadstick.*) Is he the one with the wonky bits from Tesco's? He was nice.

NIGEL   That's him. Look at that picture, it's amazing. Very bright – it's quite David LaChapelle, I think.

JAMIE   Why do you keep all these pictures, there's hundreds of them?

NIGEL   It's arty. I'm interested in the different styles of
        photography. (*Little pause.* JAMIE *stares at him.*) I
        am. Some have got cheap little webcams, some
        have taken them themselves, some have got other
        people to take them. It's a whole new erotic art
        form. Look.

        (*He clicks.*)

JAMIE   Very inspiring.

NIGEL   I'll get tonight's. Hold on.

        (*Click.*)

JAMIE   Oh my God. Is that him?

NIGEL   Isn't that stunning? I tell you something – if that
        was you, I'd have that picture framed and put on
        the wall.

JAMIE   If that was me, I'd have *you* framed and put on the
        wall.

NIGEL   Have you ever seen anything quite as gorgeous?

JAMIE   Wow.

NIGEL   Just think – any minute now, that's going to come
        knocking on our front door.

        (*Beat.*)

JAMIE   Have you got any of his face?

NIGEL   Let's have a look at the gallery.

        (*Click.*)

JAMIE   The gallery? Who do you think you are – the gay
        Tony Hart?

NIGEL   They're nice, aren't they?

JAMIE   They're all the same – lovely, great veins – but where's the face shots?

NIGEL   He hasn't sent any, he's not out.

JAMIE   Oh, surprise surprise!

NIGEL   Well having face pictures is difficult for some people.

JAMIE   Yes, people who look like barnyard animals. Look at that – it's a penis, dear. We haven't got a clue what's on the other end of it! How old is this slag meant to be?

NIGEL   Seventeen.

JAMIE   Seventeen?!

NIGEL   Well, he's fit.

JAMIE   And you're a cradle-snatcher.

NIGEL   Don't over-react. We haven't had chicken for ages.

JAMIE   Well go to the KFC then! Somerfield's do it vacuum-packed. This is my flat too, and I'm telling you: seventeen is too young.

NIGEL   You're joking, aren't you? You've been to the Astoria on a Saturday night. Seventeen's a veteran in there. In G.A.Y., he'd be an O.A.P. He'd be in the corner with a walking stick telling stories about when Kylie did records you could dance to.

JAMIE   What am I talking about – seventeen is his 'Gaydar age'. He's probably halfway down the Stanna stairlift with his stuffed mother waving from the window. And this is our hot date.

NIGEL   He is hot. Look, it says 'fit . . . athletic . . . boyish'.

JAMIE   Anyone can say that, can't they!

NIGEL   He looks seventeen in the pictures!

JAMIE   It's a cock!

NIGEL   And? You can tell how old somebody is from their cock!

JAMIE   How? What do you think you do – cut a slice off and count the rings? (*Little pause.*) For goodness sake! He could be seventy-five years old!

NIGEL   Oh please, does that look like a seventy-five year old cock to you? Look at that lovely pink skin. That's healthy and young, that is. Got a lovely, warm glow to it.

JAMIE   Oh, I've heard it all, now.

NIGEL   If he was eighty, why would it look so fresh and youthful?

JAMIE   Maybe he works for Laboratoire Garnier. Either way I do not feel comfortable about this without seeing a picture of his face.

NIGEL   Well everybody else does it. It's no different from going on the heath.

JAMIE   I don't do that either. At least I can understand that's all part of the thrill. The Forrest Gump school of dating – you never know what you're gonna get. And at least you get a nice walk and a feeling you're at one with nature. If you get stuck with someone rough, you can just go, 'ooh look – there's an owl!' and make a run for it. Once someone's through the door, you can't just hide behind the rubber plant. You've got to sit them down, give them a cup of tea and a wagon wheel and make polite conversation. (*Beat.*) Call him back and tell him we've changed our minds.

NIGEL   I can't. He'll be on his way and I haven't got his number.

JAMIE   Why not?

NIGEL   You don't want me to break the rules, do you? (*Buzzer rings.*) That's him.

JAMIE   Turn out the lights, pretend we're not in. (NIGEL *pulls a face.*) We do it when my parents come round.

NIGEL   No, just get the ansaphone.

JAMIE   I'm not getting it, you get it.

NIGEL   You sound younger.

JAMIE   How old did you say we were?

NIGEL   I just knocked a couple of years off, nothing unrealistic.

JAMIE   How old?

NIGEL   Twenty-three.

JAMIE   You're thirty two. What about me?

NIGEL   Twenty-one.

JAMIE   Once he sees us he's going to know you've lied.

(*Door buzzes again. Twice.*)

NIGEL   Get it then!

JAMIE   Oh, for God's sake.

(JAMIE *drags* NIGEL *to the ansaphone*)

NIGEL   (*panicked, getting higher pitched*) No, no, no, no, no, no . . . (JAMIE *picks it up and holds it to* NIGEL'S *mouth. In faux deep, butch voice.*) Hello

... Yeah, mate ... Come up, it's the second floor. Number fifteen, mate ... Yeah, mate. (*He buzzes him in carefully and replaces the hand set.*) And I forgot to say – he's butch. He only likes straight acting men.

JAMIE   I can't believe this.

NIGEL   Is there anything else we need to do?

JAMIE   I don't know. Maybe we can get David Blaine in to make my fat, camp arse disappear?

NIGEL   Actually you could change that shirt?

JAMIE   What?!

NIGEL   Well that is really camp!

JAMIE   It's not camp!

NIGEL   It's bright and stripey. You look like a gay Zebra.

JAMIE   Just go and let this old man in.

NIGEL   He's not going to want to do anything if you look like some wacky, Timmy Mallet freak.

JAMIE   I can't be anything other than I am.

NIGEL   Just think of it as acting, you always wanted to tread the boards.

JAMIE   And tonight I am probably going to end up under them.

NIGEL   I don't care as long as you're wearing a nice shirt.

JAMIE   Fuck off!

(NIGEL *opens the door off stage.*)

NIGEL   (*deep, faux butch voice*) Alright, mate. How ya doing?

MARK   (*off*) Alright.

              (JAMIE *looks at his shirt and proudly straightens
              it. He picks up the Bacardi Breezers and takes
              them to the kitchen.*)

NIGEL   Come in then.

MARK   Cheers.

              (NIGEL *and* MARK *enter.* MARK *is seventeen and
              the epitome of a good looking desirable young
              gay man.*)

NIGEL   Have a seat.

MARK   Cheers.

              (MARK *nervously sits down on the sofa and looks
              around the flat. Do they fancy each other? Will
              MARK fancy* JAMIE? *There is an awkward silence.*)

NIGEL   This is the living room.

MARK   Yeah?

NIGEL   Yeah. Have a seat.

MARK   Cheers.

NIGEL   That's nooooo problem. (*Pause.*) You just plonk
              yourself down, straight down, bang, like a ton of
              bricks. (*Pause.*) Awwight? (MARK *stares at him.*)
              So you're true to your word, aren't you mate.

MARK   You what?

NIGEL   You look like what your profile said. Good looking.

MARK   Cheers.

NIGEL   Am I?

MARK   Am I what?

NIGEL   Am I like my profile?

MARK   Um . . . (*Little pause.*) It's a bit dark that picture,
            innit. How old did you say you were again?

NIGEL   Twenty-three.

MARK   Oh, Yeah. (MARK *looks at him suspiciously.*)
            Where's the other one then? You weren't lying
            were you? It ain't just you, is it?

NIGEL   No, no, my partner . . . mate's . . . boyfriend's in
            the other room, he'll be in in a minute.

MARK   Oh right.

NIGEL   No point in lying is there?

MARK   No mate. (*Pause.*) Croydon's nice, innit?

NIGEL   Yes it is. I like it.

MARK   Looks much better in the dark.

NIGEL   Yes, I suppose it does.

MARK   Lots of things do.

            (*Pause.* NIGEL *smiles.*)

NIGEL   So you know it, do you – Croydon.

MARK   My cousin lives next to the Church down by the
            back of the Drummond Centre, near the sofa place.

NIGEL   Oh right. Why does he live there – likes to go
            cruising in the graveyard does he?

MARK   No, he's the vicar.

NIGEL   Oh, right. Wow. (*Pause.*) Is he good looking?

MARK   Who?

NIGEL   The vicar?

MARK   Dunno.

NIGEL   You must have an idea.

MARK   I haven't thought about it. He's alright, I s'pose.

NIGEL   There you go! (*Little pause.*) Do you fancy him
            then?

            (*Little pause.*)

MARK   No.

NIGEL   Why not?

MARK   He's my cousin.

            (*Little pause.*)

NIGEL   Didn't take you long to get here then.

MARK   I got a cab.

NIGEL   Oh, yeah.

MARK   He didn't know where it was.

            (*Pause.*)

NIGEL   Right.

MARK   I had to tell him. South Croydon High Street. It's
            the street next to that place, innit. What's it
            called? Al's Halal Meat store?

NIGEL   Yeah.

MARK   Between that and the Chicken Cottage.

NIGEL   Yeah. It's up-and-coming, this part of south Croydon.

MARK   You can always get something to eat, I s'pose. No matter what time of the night it is. Chicken, kebabs, chips, the lot.

NIGEL   The *Evening Standard ES Magazine* says it's the new Manhattan. (*Beat.*) Manhattan in New York ...

(*Pause.* MARK *stares at* NIGEL.)

MARK   They're taking the fuckin' piss, in't they?

NIGEL   Yeah thanks, maybe. Anyway. You've been up here before, have you?

MARK   That's right.

NIGEL   How comes?

MARK   I like fried chicken.

(JAMIE *walks back in and is surprised to see someone so good-looking.*)

JAMIE   Fuck me!

(*Pause.*)

MARK   . . . What?

JAMIE   You shouldn't eat too much chicken. Greasy. Clogs up your arteries.

MARK   I take the skin off first.

JAMIE   That's the way to do it.

NIGEL   What?

MARK   What?

NIGEL   What are you talking about?

JAMIE	You're very young, aren't you?
MARK	Seventeen, mate. Is that a problem?
JAMIE	No! Not at all! I mean, not for us. That's fine, that's good, good. Lucky you. (*Beat.*) Lucky us. I mean, very nice, for you, congratulations, well done youth! You! You being the youth. That is a BIG achievement, being that young. So Nigel, aren't you going to introduce me to your friend?
NIGEL	Oh God, sorry, I am SO rude.

(JAMIE *laughs nervously.*)

NIGEL	Cumboy17, this is the other half of HotholesCroydon. HotholesCroydon, Cumboy17.
JAMIE	Hi.
MARK	Hi.
JAMIE	I'm just one of the hot holes. Hot hole. . . . singular. (*Beat.*) He's the other one . . . the other hole.

(JAMIE *puts his hand out to shake it.* MARK *looks nervous but takes it.*)

NIGEL	I'm Nigel and this is Jamie.
MARK	My name's Mark.
NIGEL	(*giggly*) Oh right Mark. Hi 'Mark'. How funny.
MARK	What's funny about it?
NIGEL	I just didn't think of you as having a name, silly really but I thought of you just as Cumboy17. Ridiculous, really but I suppose all I was doing was looking at your . . . (*Beat.*) . . . picture. I mean not just looking at your picture, you know because it's just a picture of your (*Delicately.*)

well, cock, isn't it, if I can say that word. (*Little pause.*) It's a very nice one, as they go but there's more to you than just your (*Coyly.*) 'picture' isn't there? I mean, there is – we saw all your interests on your profile. Favourite food, favourite film, everything you need to know . . .

MARK   Yeah.

NIGEL   Your favourite actress is Jessie Wallace and your favourite country is Magaluf and you 'don't take no shit from no mother-fucker', apparently. Quite right. As my mother always used to say.

MARK   I didn't look at yours.

JAMIE   That's alright. Why would you? So, erm . . . make yourself at home. Kick back, relax. Can I get you a drink or something? Cup of coffee?

NIGEL   Cappuccino if you want, we've got a machine.

MARK   Nah, too poncy.

NIGEL   Something stronger?

JAMIE   Jack Daniels? Vodka? . . . Ribena Toothkind?

MARK   What's that?

JAMIE   Nothing. Coke?

MARK   Yeah, Coke.

JAMIE   What would you like, dear? (*Coughs.*) Nigel?

NIGEL   I'll have a Rolling Rock.

JAMIE   A what?

NIGEL   Rolling Rock. It's a type of beer.

JAMIE   Yes, I know what it is but we haven't got any Rolling Rock. Have we?

NIGEL   Yes, we have. They're in the kitchen, where we always keep the beer.

JAMIE   Oh, yes. (JAMIE *stands there.*) Can you just remind me – where is that?

NIGEL   In the cabinet . . . above the microwave. With the paint and my power drill.

JAMIE   Oh right, yeah.

NIGEL   (*laughing*) He can be a bit of a wanker sometimes.

JAMIE   I heard that. I'd be careful if I were you, (*Emphasises word.*) darling.

NIGEL   It's probably old age. That's what blokes are like, innit. Silly bastard. (*Off,* JAMIE *laughs out loud in a prolonged way.*) He's losing his mind.

JAMIE   Looks that way, doesn't it. Me and Liza Minelli both. (*Sings.*) I'm losing my mind . . .

NIGEL   (*shouting*) Shut up! (NIGEL *snaps back to* MARK *with a cheesy, semi-embarrassed grin on his face.* MARK *and* NIGEL *sit in a prolonged awkward silence.*) Shall I put some music on?

MARK   If you want.

NIGEL   What do you like?

MARK   Got any Eminem?

NIGEL   Don't think so. Isn't he homophobic?

MARK   Who gives a shit. I like R 'n' B, Fifty Cent, Snoop Dogg . . .

NIGEL   That's nice. (*Beat.*) People used to think I was black. (*Beat.*) From my voice. (MARK *stares.*) We haven't got any R 'n' B, sorry.

MARK   What else you got?

NIGEL   Let me see . . .

                (NIGEL *gets up and goes to the shelves of CDs.*)

MARK   I hate it when gays always like the same shit music. Just 'cos I fancy blokes doesn't mean I have to like Abba and all that shit, does it? I went to this bloke's flat once and all he had was Britney, Kylie and soundtracks of musicals. Put me right off him.

                (*He picks up a wedge of about twenty CDs en-masse from the shelf and drops them into an open drawer and slams it shut.*)

NIGEL   Actually, let's not have music.

MARK   Whatever.

                (NIGEL *comes and sits back down.*)

NIGEL   So. Do you live far?

MARK   Sanderstead.

NIGEL   Oh yeah, right of course – and you got a cab. So that's a horny pic on your profile then.

                (*Pause.*)

MARK   What?

NIGEL   Your Gaydar pic . . .

MARK   Oh yeah. Cheers.

NIGEL   Cumboy17. That's good. I really like that. How did you think of that then?

                (*Pause.* MARK *looks up at* NIGEL *like he's stupid.*)

MARK   Well . . . I like cum . . . I'm a boy . . .

(*Little pause.*)

NIGEL   Yes?

MARK   And I'm seventeen.

NIGEL   Oh yeah, clever.

          (JAMIE *enters with beers and a plates of biscuits.*)

JAMIE   Here you go.

          (*He hands* NIGEL *his beer.*)

JAMIE   Hold it. Up. (*He opens it then opens his own.*)
          There. Oops. There you go. (*Beat.*) Fig roll?

MARK   Did you bake 'em yourself?

JAMIE   I'm sorry?

MARK   Did you cook 'em? I only like home baking. Don't
          like that Tesco's shit.

JAMIE   Oh right. No, sorry.

MARK   Gotta be moist, gotta be fresh, gotta be done
          properly. Not packaged in shitty plastic. I'm
          gonna be a chef, I am.

NIGEL   Is that what you do for a living then, Mark?

MARK   Not yet.

JAMIE   Are you at college?

MARK   No. I'm a waiter in the Toby Inn in Sanderstead.

NIGEL   Oh OK, yeah I know it. Where they do the never-
          ending custard jug. As much custard as you can
          eat.

MARK   That's it. You been there?

NIGEL   Yeah. We went there for your mum's 60th?

JAMIE   That wasn't a Toby Inn.

NIGEL   It was.

JAMIE   No, it wasn't.

NIGEL   It was. The one with the fit waiter.

JAMIE   That was that place in Shirley we went to for my mum's 60th.

NIGEL   It was the Toby Inn. The waiter kept eyeing me up. I was the one who booked it.

JAMIE   You were not!

NIGEL   Yes I was. It's not like I was particularly thrilled about the idea of going to a carvery or whatever they're called but we needed a change. If I left it to him we'd never step out of Pizza Express, would we? Honestly, it's a nightmare – his idea of adventurous dining is to not have the Fiorentina. Although, no offence, the Toby Inn's not that cutting edge is it? I prefer to eat in town.

MARK   Is that right?

NIGEL   That's why I remember it was the Toby Inn for his mother's birthday. Full of old dears, it was. But they liked it, bless them. Give them a piece of carrot cake and they think they've died and gone to Claridges. (*Getting into his stride.*) It's a carrot and it's a pudding! Wow, you've blown my mind! (*Laughs at his own joke.*) I wanted to go to the Wolesley. The food in there is incredible. Jamie, can you imagine it with your mum and her friends in there? It would have been like putting pearls before swine.

JAMIE   Please don't embarrass me. He always starts showing off the minute we have company. No one's impressed – I'm not, he's not, are you slutboy?

MARK   Cumboy.

JAMIE   See.

NIGEL   Now, now. We don't want to start rowing in front of our guest now, do we.

JAMIE   No we don't. Would you like another drink?

MARK   No.

JAMIE   It was actually a gastropub in Shirley. I booked it, he never books them.

NIGEL   Whatever, we went to the Toby Inn one time and the waiter couldn't take his eyes off me. (*Beat.*) Was that you then?

          (*Pause.*)

MARK   No.

          (*Pause.*)

JAMIE   So, do you live with your mum and dad?

MARK   No, they don't like gays.

JAMIE   Oh, don't they? I'm sorry to hear that. They'll come round.

MARK   No it's alright. They're a pair of bastards.

JAMIE   Oh, I take it you don't get on then?

MARK   They threw me out.

NIGEL   I don't get on with my parents either, my mum. You soon forget about it.

MARK   I have.

NIGEL   Water off a duck's back. (*Little pause.*) She called me the C-word, once, my mum. I've never liked that word. You hear it all the time these days but it still freaks me out. I hate it. I will not have the C-word in this flat . . .

(*Little pause.*)

MARK   The C-word?

JAMIE   Carbohydrate.

NIGEL   No . . . (*Glaring at* JAMIE, *with hushed voice.*) cunt. I know everyone uses it these days but they didn't when I was young. You don't expect to hear that word from your mother, especially when it's about you, to you. Haven't spoken to her since.

(*Pause.*)

MARK   Not at all?

NIGEL   No big deal.

JAMIE   It's alright if it is, Nige.

NIGEL   No, her loss. Good excuse not to have a crap Christmas, isn't it. Family bloody values. Don't make me laugh. The family have done nothing but shit on gay people from day one. (JAMIE *looks up and acknowledges this.*) So where do you live now then?

MARK   With my best mate Karen.

NIGEL   And she's cool with the gay thing?

MARK   I'm not gay, mate. (*Pause.*) I'm Bi. Bi-curious.

JAMIE   Aha.

NIGEL   Oh, are you?

MARK   Is that a problem?

NIGEL   No, it's fantastic. A real man!

JAMIE   Ugh.

MARK   I mess around with blokes but I know I'll get
        married one day. Prefer women. Men are just a side
        thing. See I'm not like you. (*Beat.*) I like cunt.

        (*Pause. Embarrassed silence.*)

JAMIE   But I bet you couldn't eat a whole one, right?
        (*Beat.*) Butter Finger, anyone?

        (*Pause.*)

MARK   No thanks..

NIGEL   So I'll bet you get a lot of interest off of Gaydar,
        don't you.

MARK   I do alright.

NIGEL   More than alright I expect.

MARK   Mainly posh blokes.

JAMIE   Really?

Mark   Telling me how much money they've got 'cos they
        think it'll impress me. Some geezer who lived in the
        countryside near Crawley said he was gonna drive
        up here and get me and take me to his house. He
        wanted me to come and stay with 'im. Asked me if
        I'd go bareback with 'im. (*Beat.*) I don't wanna go
        bareback. I hate horses! (*Little pause.*) Fuckin'
        horrible, smelly things! They eat 'em in France.
        They taste nice, 'pparently. No offence, but why
        can't I meet no one normal?

JAMIE   It's difficult.

NIGEL   Great to be popular, though. You must have met a few of them?

MARK   Not many. (*Beat.*) One or two.

NIGEL   Anyone nice?

MARK   Kinda.

NIGEL   Yeah?

MARK   Went out with one.

NIGEL   Did you?

MARK   He was a liar. Saw his profile. Said he was fit. Said he was 28, said lots of things. Went to meet him. He was dead posh bloke an' all. He was 42 and married.

NIGEL   Oh God, that's awful.

MARK   Yeah.

JAMIE   People lying. Very bad. Especially about their age.

MARK   No. It wasn't his age that bothered me. He told me he loved me. He lied when he said he loved me. (*Pause.*) He said he would leave his wife. He said he loved me, he said he'd look after me, he said a lot of things. Then couple of months later he stopped saying anything. They always say they'll leave but they don't though, do they?

JAMIE   I don't s'pose they do.

MARK   It's alright. I don't care or nuffin'. Just learnt that the only one you can rely on is in this world is yourself.

    (*Pause.*)

JAMIE   Well, it's been lovely, hasn't it but it's getting on . . . maybe we should/

(*Pause.*)

NIGEL So then. (*Little pause.*) What shall we do now?

JAMIE (*cringing*) Oh no.

NIGEL Are you thinking what we're thinking?

MARK Y'what?

NIGEL You wanna go in the other room and have a little bit of adult fun, mate?

JAMIE (*cringing*) Adult fun?

(JAMIE *puts his hand over his face in embarrassment.*)

MARK Erm . . . (*Little pause.*) Can I use your loo?

NIGEL Yeah, just out there – first on the left. Next to the bedroom.

(*They sit in silence as* MARK *goes out.* JAMIE *glares at* NIGEL.)

NIGEL What's the matter?

JAMIE I don't like this.

NIGEL Why not?

JAMIE It's ridiculous, he's not into it.

NIGEL Stop panicking.

JAMIE It's midnight, it's our anniversary and there's some strange boy in the bathroom . . . who doesn't want to be here! And neither do I quite frankly.

NIGEL Oh, it's fantastic, he's so common, I can't believe it. He's a proper chav. It's like he just stepped off of the council estate!

JAMIE   And as soon as he's had a piss he'll be stepping right back there.

NIGEL   Have you seen the way he talks? (*Shudders with delight.*) Ohhh, it's amazing. It's like some Triga video come to life. I love it! You don't know whether he's going to fuck us or mug us!

JAMIE   Well, don't get excited. We are obviously not his type.

NIGEL   Of course we are. He's just shy. We just need to get him in the mood, maybe he's hungry.

JAMIE   He's already turned his nose up at my Soft Baked Be Good to Yourselfs.

NIGEL   Were you listening? He only likes home baking! Haven't we got any fresh cookies or muffins?

JAMIE   No, we fired Nigella last week.

NIGEL   There must be some Kit Kats in the tin. Go and have a look. We can put some out.

JAMIE   Yes that's a good idea. We can make a trail back to the bedroom. (*Beat.*) And find some puppies to lure him in with. And then I'll get the candy floss machine out and put my clown suit on and if you can find your Billy doll we can put on a puppet show.

NIGEL   Shut up.

JAMIE   And you can drive our ice cream van round and we can see if we can find a Wendy House with a glory hole in it!

NIGEL   Stop being stupid and think of something! (*Beat.*) Why don't we put some music on? We must have something that's young and current . . .

JAMIE   Yes!

NIGEL	What?
JAMIE	Steps Gold?!
NIGEL	Yes! (*Beat.*) No!
JAMIE	Why not?
NIGEL	They're not current – they split up two years ago!
JAMIE	Well, Lisa-fucking-Scott-Lee then!
NIGEL	Jamie, don't use that word in front of me!
JAMIE	Lisa Scott-Lee?
NIGEL	No, fuck! Why does every word you speak have to be an obscenity? It's offensive!
JAMIE	Nigel, you've been on-line all night with a complete stranger telling him you want to stick your tongue up his arse, this is hardly the time to start coming over all Mary Whitehouse!
NIGEL	He might not be comfortable with that kind of language. Not everybody is, you know.
JAMIE	Nigel, he's not Julie Andrews – he's called Cumboy17!
NIGEL	Keep your voice down, he'll hear you.
JAMIE	Fuck him! And fuck you!
NIGEL	Oh very nice – on our anniversary – how romantic.
JAMIE	Oh sorry, Barbara Cartland! Shame we can't all be as lovey dovey as you are – arranging a party, champagne and a teenager named after his obsession with semen to come over and pop his cork in our faces! (*Beat.*) I would have been happy with a cake! And just when we finally had an

excuse to actually buy something from Patisserie bloody Valerie.

NIGEL   Be quiet!

JAMIE   What's he doing in there anyway? He's taking forever.

NIGEL   He's from Sanderstead. He's probably trying to chisel off the fittings.

JAMIE   I wish he'd just make up his mind and just . . . oh.

         (MARK *steps through. He is in his underwear.*)

MARK   I can't wait all night, lads. Are you gonna fuck me or what?

         (JAMIE *looks shocked.*)

JAMIE   Ohhhhhh . . .

NIGEL   . . . K. (NIGEL *gets up and goes over to* MARK *and he runs his hand up* MARK'S *body and over his chest.*) You're really fit, mate.

         (*They start to kiss passionately.* MARK *undoes* NIGEL'S *jeans.*)

JAMIE   Nigel. Wait. I don't know if I . . .

NIGEL   Be quiet.

JAMIE   Nigel. I'm not sure if I . . .

         (MARK *looks up and beckons* JAMIE *over.*)

NIGEL   Put some music on.

JAMIE   (*under his breath*) What music?

NIGEL   Anything!

(JAMIE *presses the button on the remote control.
You by S Club blasts out.* MARK *and* NIGEL *stop
and stare at* JAMIE *who, flustered, presses the
button on the remote control. He presses it again
and the chorus of Buenos Aires by Madonna from
Evita blares out.* JAMIE *drops the remote control,
picks it up, presses a button again and another,
faster, darker hard-core dance track begins. They
get it together. Fade to black. Music gets louder
and continues.*)

Scene Two

JAMIE *and* NIGEL'S *flat. Interior. Saturday morning. 9.45 AM.*
JAMIE *enters slowly and looks at the clothes on the floor.*

JAMIE   Oh God. (*He goes to the kitchen.*) Tea or coffee?

             (MARK *enters with his arms wrapped round
             himself. He stands and looks around the flat
             longingly at* JAMIE.)

             Who wants tea, who wants coffee?

             (JAMIE *walks in and into* MARK.)

MARK   Boo.

JAMIE   Oh, sorry. Tea or coffee?

MARK   Tea please. Milky.

JAMIE   I think they're your things there. It was all a bit
             mad last night.

             (*Beat.*)

MARK   I like mad.

JAMIE   (*embarrassed*) Yes. Good. Great. Very nice. (*Beat.*)
             Do you take sugar?

MARK   Two please.

JAMIE   Nige, what do you want?

NIGEL   (*off*) Coffee, please.

               (JAMIE *goes into the kitchen.* MARK *gathers his clothes on the floor and starts to dress.*)

JAMIE   Nigel. Did you get any milk?

               (NIGEL *enters. He puts his arms round* MARK.)

NIGEL   Oh shit no, sorry.

JAMIE   Well we haven't got any. We'll have to get breakfast in town.

NIGEL   We can't do that when we've got a guest here. Do you want some cereal? I can go and get some milk.

JAMIE   No, no it's fine, don't worry . . .

NIGEL   I'll be five minutes.

JAMIE   Great.

NIGEL   I'll go up the shop then.

JAMIE   If you're going can you get some food for Robbie as well. Get Beef IAMs, not that cheap stuff.

               (NIGEL *picks up his things on the floor and gets dressed.*)

NIGEL   You want anything?

MARK   I'm alright, thanks.

JAMIE   So, are you going to Pride this year?

MARK   No, not me.

NIGEL   Shame. Why not?

MARK   They don't know about me at work. I couldn't risk
            being seen there.

JAMIE   Who would see you?

MARK   There's a couple of 'em there are gays.

JAMIE   Oh.

NIGEL   All that political stuff puts kids off, I think.

JAMIE   What political stuff? There is none.

NIGEL   Peter bloody Tatchell. You don't want to end up
            like him, do you.

JAMIE   Don't let's start on him again.

NIGEL   All right! I'm going to go before it all kicks off.

JAMIE   Good idea.

NIGEL   Oh, one more thing . . .

JAMIE   What?

            (*Pause.*)

NIGEL   Happy Anniversary.

JAMIE   Oh yeah, Happy Anniversary.

            (*They kiss;* JAMIE *self-consciously. There is an
            awkward silence.*)

NIGEL   I love you.

JAMIE   Love you, too.

NIGEL   See you in a minute.

            (NIGEL *picks up his keys and leaves.*)

JAMIE   So . . . erm . . . do you want some cereal or
           something? Something to eat? We've got
           Weetabix, Alpen . . . ?

MARK   No milk for cereal.

JAMIE   Oh yeah, shit. Toast?

MARK   Yeah.

JAMIE   Yeah?

MARK   Sure.

           (JAMIE *goes out to kitchen.*)

MARK   That was fun last night. I've never had a
           threesome as good as that before.

JAMIE   (*shouting from kitchen*) How many bits?

MARK   (*mis-hearing him*) Was really, really horny.

JAMIE   (*shouting from kitchen*) Is two bits enough for
           you?

MARK   Oh yeah, my mouths not big enough to get three
           in at the same time. I ain't Will Young you know!

JAMIE   No, two bits. Of toast. (*Beat.*) Is-two-bits-of-toast-
           enough-for-you?

MARK   Oh sorry, yeah. Yes. Yes please.

           (JAMIE *comes back in.*)

MARK   Sorry. Didn't mean to embarrass you.

JAMIE   (*embarrassed*) You didn't embarrass me. I'm not
           embarrassed.

MARK   Is it your anniversary today then?

JAMIE   Yes. We met at Pride '95 – the date changes so we
               always celebrate it on Pride Day. Seems like a
               good excuse.

MARK   Yeah.

               (*Pause.*)

JAMIE   So. It'll be a nice walk.

MARK   What?

JAMIE   For Nigel. Him. It'll be a nice walk for him. Just
               round the corner. Looks like it'll be pretty sunny
               for today.

MARK   Oh yeah. You're gonna be late for your Gay Pride.
               What time does it start?

JAMIE   Eleven I think. I can't remember where exactly –
               they keep changing it.

MARK   There lots of people there? Gay people?

JAMIE   Yeah, thousands. It's weird when you first go. It's
               the one day of the year where you can put a dress
               on and wear some lipstick, eyeliner, high heels,
               really go the whole hog. (*Beat.*) It is just one day
               of the year. (*Beat.*) If that's what the lesbians
               wanna do.

MARK   What?

JAMIE   They've got to have one day off from being under
               the ground driving those trains, haven't they.
               They come out blinking into the sun like little gay
               moles.

MARK   What you on about, mate?

JAMIE   The lesbians . . . ? I'm joking. No? OK. So Mardi
               Gras, Pride, whatever it's called, it's fun. It's the
               best day of the year. It's amazing. Gay people
               everywhere. 360 degrees. Can you imagine that,

it's great. It's a bit 'I see gay people' but you get over that.

(*The toaster pops.*)

I better get that. (*From the kitchen.*) You should come today. You'd probably enjoy it. Come with us. If you want to.

MARK   No thanks. I ain't one for screamin' and shoutin' about it. It's nobody's business but mine. No offence. I fancy men but I ain't like the rest of them, all camp. I hate that. I'm just a normal bloke that does normal things that just happen to fancy other blokes.

JAMIE   Fair enough. (*Beat.*) What do you want on your toast – butter?

MARK   No way. Only eat Bertorelli – it's the new name for Olivio. It's the only one that's only fifty nine percent fat with only fourteen grams of saturated fat for every hundred grams.

JAMIE   Oh right.

MARK   14.5 grams of polyunsaturates.

JAMIE   We've only got Sainsburys own – and Jam, lemon curd, marmite . . .

MARK   Like a marmite miner?

JAMIE   A what?

MARK   Marmite miner? You know. (*Points to his bottom.*) You know. (*Whistles and then laughs.*)

JAMIE   Yeah. (*Forces laugh.*)

MARK   Just the marg, please.

JAMIE   OK.

(*Pause.*)

MARK   Nice flat, innit.

JAMIE   Yeah, I'm happy with it.

MARK   You been living here long?

JAMIE   Yeah just under nine years.

MARK   You buy it together?

JAMIE   No, he got it a few months after I met him – money
            from when his dad died went towards it – before
            he came out to his mum. I moved in just after a
            year.

MARK   So it's his then?

JAMIE   Well, both of ours really. I've actually paid more
            of the mortgage than he is. He's been out of work
            a few times.

MARK   What does he do?

JAMIE   Works in PR.

MARK   What's that?

JAMIE   Public relations. Looking after people's brands.
            Making you think you want things you don't.

MARK   Yeah he's good at that.

            (*They pause, embarrassed.*)

JAMIE   It's a good job. Looks after the PR for some big
            high street shops. He's never been completely
            sure what he wants to do, really. Just goes in,
            does his bit, e-mails me pictures of porn stars.
            Sent me a great one of Justin Timberlake fucking
            Johan Paulik the other day. Lives for the weekend,
            really.

MARK   We all do.

(Pause.)

JAMIE   Yeah, he's a bit of a party animal . . . (JAMIE *notices* MARK *is looking at him wide-eyed.*) What?

MARK   Is Justin Timberlake gay then?

JAMIE   No, no, they're just fake pictures off the internet.

MARK   I think he is, though. My mate knows someone who used to go out with him when he worked in America. (JAMIE *smiles.*) He did. I've seen the pictures.

JAMIE   OK. I hope he is.

MARK   So do I.

(Pause.)

JAMIE   Do you go out a lot then?

MARK   Yeah. I've been to a few places. The Goose and Carrot.

JAMIE   Oh yeah . . .

MARK   And Bar Ego . . .

JAMIE   In West Norwood. Did you like it?

MARK   Yeah, it was alright. I just don't like those gays much. Everyone's just after one thing.

JAMIE   Well, not everyone.

MARK   S'pose so. I just think it's a bit odd that there are always the same people there whenever I go. And you see these people trying to get off with different people every week. Everyone knows everyone and everyone gossips and they all call each other girl's names and know everyone else's business. They're really weird half of 'em an' all. I don't like being in places full of old people.

JAMIE   Well, that's a good thing about the gay scene. It's diverse. Very cosmopolitan. It's where young and old mix. All different kinds and types of people all getting along and having a fabulous time together . . . all getting on . . . (*Beat.*) Another drink?

MARK   I'm OK. I just think I don't wanna be going to dancing to S Club when I'm thirty trying to pick up young boys all the time. I see these sad bastards running round being bitchy and camp and I think isn't it about time you grew out of that? If I get to be like that when I'm thirty I want someone to shoot me. (*Pause.*) How old are you?

JAMIE   Thirty.

MARK   Well you look a bit younger, so it's alright.

JAMIE   Yes.

MARK   Not twenty-one then?

JAMIE   No.

MARK   Didn't think so.

JAMIE   Sorry. We got a bit carried away.

MARK   It's alright, I'm used to it. I like older blokes.

JAMIE   Do you?

MARK   Some.

(*Little pause.*)

JAMIE   How's your toast?

MARK   It's fine. Thanks. (*Pause.*) So, do you do it a lot then, threesomes?

JAMIE   Every now and then. It depends if we like someone. Not that much. Mostly we don't.

MARK   'Cos I've seen Nigel's profile on Gaydar quite a lot.

JAMIE   What do you mean?

MARK   On-line every weekend.

JAMIE   Well he just has it on sometimes. Just to look.

MARK   And in the week as well sometimes.

JAMIE   I like to look as well – we both do – but I don't have a profile. He does it mainly. I can't be arsed, I don't really know how it works . . .

MARK   God.

JAMIE   What?

MARK   You must be really trusting.

JAMIE   Why?

MARK   Well you can't be a jealous person if you don't mind seeing someone with your boyfriend.

JAMIE   Well you know it's only sex. It's me he loves and we don't do it that often. (*Pause.*) And we have a great relationship.

MARK   Seems like it.

JAMIE   We do. It's our tenth anniversary today.

MARK   Yeah I heard.

JAMIE   And we have rules.

MARK   Rules?

JAMIE	About what we do and what we don't do.
MARK	Like what?
JAMIE	Well we have to both fancy the person.
MARK	That's always a good start.
JAMIE	We never sleep with anyone unless we really, really like them.
MARK	You are romantic then.
JAMIE	We never give them our phone number or either of our mobile numbers. We never take their number. Ever. We never do anything when the other person isn't there.
MARK	OK.
JAMIE	We always wear a condom and vice versa. Only safe sex. That's really, really important.
MARK	You didn't last night.
JAMIE	We did with you. We don't on our own.
MARK	He tried to do it to me without a condom.
JAMIE	He was just drunk and over excited. He did stop.
MARK	Only when you slapped him. Twice. And then started screaming.
JAMIE	Well. He never would have carried on.
MARK	So you must've really both liked me then last night? To fuck me?
JAMIE	I suppose so. Yes.
MARK	Anything else?
JAMIE	And we only ever see the person once.

MARK   Oh, right. Why's that?

JAMIE   It's better that way.

MARK   (*lights up*) In case one of you has an affair?

JAMIE   An affair. That's old fashioned word. No, no one's going to have an affair. I trust him and he trusts me.

MARK   So why not see someone again then if you like having sex with 'em?

JAMIE   Well, best to put things out of harm's reach, don't you think?

MARK   And you stick to the rules do you?

JAMIE   Yes. Definitely.

            (MARK *nods cynically.*)

MARK   Fair enough I s'pose.

            (*Pause.*)

JAMIE   It's quite romantic really.

MARK   Romantic?

JAMIE   Yeah.

MARK   Oh, come on! It's not romantic, is it?

JAMIE   Yes it is!

MARK   It's a lot of things but romantic isn't one of them.

JAMIE   And you'd know?

MARK   It's your anniversary and you're with someone else!

JAMIE   It's not as simple as that . . .

MARK   Well actually it is, isn't it? If I loved someone I
          wouldn't want them sleeping with anyone else full
          stop.

JAMIE   Well it might seem like that when you're young, to
          someone who has never had a proper relationship.

MARK   Fuck off, 'because I'm young'! That don't mean
          nothing. I'm young but I know what going out
          with someone means . . .

JAMIE   . . . of course you do.

MARK   . . . and I'd rather not have a boyfriend at all than
          have one like this. It's pathetic!

JAMIE   Oh right. Well, thank you very much for your
          advice, Kilroy-Silk.

MARK   Kilroy-Silk. What's that? Some kind of lubricant?

JAMIE   Not exactly.

MARK   Don't you get it free with condoms?

JAMIE   Well, you'd definitely feel ripped off if you paid
          for it . . . anyway, doesn't matter – I just mean you
          just don't really know what you're talking about –
          things change as you get older.

MARK   Yeah that's right – your balls drop . . . and yours
          have dropped off. Don't tell me you're all loved up
          and romantic, because I know you ain't!

JAMIE   What do you mean, 'you know I ain't?'

MARK   You know what I'm talking about.

JAMIE   I haven't got a clue what you're talking/

MARK   You wouldn't have kissed me like you did last
          night.

JAMIE	What?
MARK	You wouldn't have been as turned on as you were if you wanted to be with him.
JAMIE	We were having sex!
MARK	The way you touched me when we were in bed – you sent an electric shock right through me.
JAMIE	I think it was the duvet. It's a polyester mix.
MARK	No, no, it's more than that. I can tell you want me. (*Pause.*) Just like I want you.
JAMIE	Mark, you've already had me. Believe me – there's not that much more to have.
MARK	I'd like to see you again.
JAMIE	What?
MARK	We could be fuck buddies.
JAMIE	Fuck buddies?
MARK	I could come round here whenever he's out at work, you could/
JAMIE	Hold on a minute . . .
MARK	/You could fuck me whenever you want. Here, my place, wherever. I have someone else who just comes over same time, same day every week. I leave the door open, he doesn't speak, doesn't kiss me, I don't even know who he is . . . just holds me down and fucks me.
JAMIE	Charming.
MARK	And you could, too. You could do whatever you want – just hold me by the ears and fuck my head.
JAMIE	I think someone's beaten me to it.

Mark   What?

Jamie   I just mean you must be out of your mind if you're
            doing that kind of thing. It's dangerous. Jesus,
            you're seventeen. You should be screeching at
            people in Old Compton Street and sleeping with
            Westlife fans and going out with hairdressers, not
            chasing round old farts like me.

Mark   You're not an old fart. You're thirty. I liked it with
            you. You're good in bed. You're nice. You're a
            nice guy. And you're dead sexy.

Jamie   Mark . . .

Mark   It's simple, innit.

Jamie   I'm too old for you.

            (Mark *pushes himself onto* Jamie.)

Mark   Well you know what they say in the gay world . . .

Jamie   What? What do they say?

Mark   You're as old as the man you feel.

            (Mark *takes* Jamie's *hand and presses against his
            crotch. Then* Jamie *pulls away.*)

Jamie   This is wrong.

Mark   No it ain't.

Jamie   Nigel will be back in a minute.

Mark   It doesn't matter if he comes back in, we'll hear
            him.

Jamie   No. What if we don't. He might go mad and
            anything could happen.

Mark   Just kiss me. (Mark *pulls* Jamie *into a kiss again.*)
            You know you want to.

(MARK *starts to undo* JAMIE'S *belt.*)

JAMIE   (*gently*) No . . .

MARK   I want you to fuck me right now. Gone on – fuck me over the sofa!

JAMIE   No, I can't!!

MARK   Why not?

JAMIE   It's from Habitat.

(*Pause.*)

MARK   For fuck's sake!

JAMIE   It's from the spring 2005 Ektorp range, I'd cum to quick.

MARK   Will you stop being so gay?

JAMIE   I don't care if you're Tom Cruise, you'd have to kell me before I let you make a mess on my Ektorp.

MARK   Let's just got to the bedroom then, he'll never know.

JAMIE   No, no, no, I'm sorry I can't do this, it's against the rules . . .

MARK   Sod the rules!

JAMIE   No, I won't.

MARK   Why not?!

JAMIE   Because I love my boyfriend!

MARK   You just think you do.

JAMIE   Will you stop telling me what I think? You don't know me. Actually I do, I do love him.

MARK   But he treats you so badly.

JAMIE   Well you don't walk out the minute the going gets tough. We've been together for ten years and I'm in love with him. Yes we fuck around and no maybe I don't always like it, and yes, so I give in to what hc wants a lot of the time but I wouldn't put up with it if I didn't love him.

MARK   But I . . . I . . .

           (*Pause.*)

JAMIE   Look, I'm very flattered that you like me – you're very young, and very good looking and there'll be queues of nice men falling over themselves to go out with you, but it won't be me.

MARK   You're meant to jump at the chance of going out with me. Who the fuck do you think you are? I'm seventeen. Soon as they see that on Gaydar they're all over me. They all want to fuck me. What's the matter with you?

JAMIE   Calm down!

MARK   You won't get another chance like this. I'm young, Who'd want you?

JAMIE   Stop it! Mark, I've been seventeen. I'm not worried about getting older. It's called growing up. I have a boyfriend who I love. Yes I do. I know that's not want you want to hear but it's the truth. I'm sorry.

           (*Pause.*)

MARK   I'm sorry.

JAMIE   No, I'm sorry. It's fine. It doesn't matter. I am SO flattered, you have no idea. A good looking boy like you, coming on to me. Listen, why don't you come to Pride today?

MARK   No, you're alright. It's not my thing. I can't see much to be proud of really.

JAMIE   What do you mean?

MARK   Well, look at you. You're going to Gay Pride. Maybe you could get some pride in yourself.

JAMIE   That's not fair.

MARK   Well nothing is, is it. You're a bunch of tossers the lot of you. You're all the same, gay people. You come in, you say this and that, you act like you give a fuck – oh, I'll take you under my wing, oh, I'll be your friend, I'll show you around, help you get to know how everything works – and then as soon as you get what you want you just fuck off. If I knew everyone would be like this then I wouldn't have bothered coming out in the first place.

JAMIE   That's not fair . . .

MARK   Look, please, I'll message you on Gaydar and we can meet up again.

JAMIE   I don't see those messages, it's Nigel's profile. I don't have one of my own.

MARK   Well why don't you get one then – it only takes two minutes.

JAMIE   I don't want to!

MARK   Well, I'll give you my number then!

JAMIE   Mark, no, please . . .

MARK   Look, just call me. I'll give you my mobile, you can call me anytime you want and I'll be there . . .

(MARK *grabs a pen and a piece of paper and scribbles his number down.*)

JAMIE	We've been through this, it's not going to happen.
MARK	Just take my number!
JAMIE	I won't call you.
MARK	For fuck's sake!

(JAMIE *panics and stuffs the piece of paper with* MARK'S *number on it into his pocket. He arranges his T-shirt and trousers.* NIGEL *enters just as* MARK *arranges himself.*)

NIGEL	That shop always tries to overcharge me. You alright boys?
JAMIE	Yeah.
NIGEL	Getting to know each other better?
MARK	Something like that.
JAMIE	Did you get milk?

(NIGEL *holds up a pint of milk.*)

NIGEL	What do you think this is – Scotch mist?
JAMIE	What about cat food?
NIGEL	Oh shit.

(*Pause.*)

JAMIE	Doesn't matter, I'll give him tuna.
NIGEL	That cat eats better than I do.
JAMIE	He's your cat.
MARK	I haven't seen your cat. Where's your cat?
JAMIE	Out. (*Pause.*) Well, I was thinking: it's getting on. We're going to be late for the march.

NIGEL   We've got plenty of time yet.

JAMIE   No, we should be getting on.

NIGEL   You don't have to leave so soon. I'm sure we've got time for another cup of coffee . . .

MARK   I need to go home.

NIGEL   How are you gonna get back?

MARK   I don't know. It's ages from here. Where's the station?

NIGEL   You have to walk up to East Croydon.

JAMIE   We'll give you a lift up there if you want.

MARK   You will?

JAMIE   Nigel will.

NIGEL   I will?

JAMIE   Yes, you will. Go on Nige, now or we'll be late. Then you can get some Whiskas from the garage.

MARK   You don't have to, I can walk.

NIGEL   No it's fine. Come on then, cutie.

JAMIE   Well, it was nice meeting you.

MARK   Yeah, nice meeting you. I would ask for your number but I know it's against the rules.

(*Pause.*)

NIGEL   Oh you've been told about 'The Rules', have you?

MARK   Yeah, I know all about the rules.

JAMIE   So, really nice meeting you.

(JAMIE *gives* MARK *a kiss and a hug.*)

JAMIE	Everything will be alright you know, it will. It always seems like a big deal when you come out ...
MARK	Yeah.
JAMIE	Did you have anything else?
MARK	Think my mobile's in the bedroom.

(MARK *exits to the bedroom.*)

NIGEL	What was that about?
JAMIE	I feel sorry for him. I think he's lonely.
NIGEL	You should be worrying about if he's nicked anything.
JAMIE	Nigel.
NIGEL	I'm serious. Where's your mobile?
JAMIE	It's over there. Will you stop!
NIGEL	You'll be saying stop when he books a holiday on your credit card. I hope you haven't left him alone with anything. He'll be down the market flogging anything he can get his hands on, working class tramp.
JAMIE	Just stop, stop it.
NIGEL	And thanks for lumbering me with him.

(*Pause.*)

JAMIE	It will take you ten minutes.
NIGEL	OK.

(*Pause.*)

JAMIE	Nige?
NIGEL	What?

JAMIE   Do you respect me?

NIGEL   Course I do.

JAMIE   No, I mean really respect me.

NIGEL   Of course I respect you. What a funny thing to say. Ten years! Don't be so stupid. Come here.

(They kiss. MARK *enters. They pull out of their embrace.)*

JAMIE   Don't you want to take your new jacket?

NIGEL   It's not cold out. Come on then, trouble.

MARK   Bye.

JAMIE   Nice to meet you.

MARK   Yeah.

NIGEL   See you in a minute.

JAMIE   Alright. Don't be long.

MARK   Have a nice day.

JAMIE   Thank you, hope so. (NIGEL *and* MARK *exit. Pause.*) It's our big day.

(Blackout. Holding Back the Years by Simply Red plays. Suddenly there's a crack of thunder and we hear the noise of rain. It stops as the lights rise on the next scene.)

Scene Three

JAMIE *enters with two cups of tea and puts one of them down on the coffee table. This scene should be tense.*

JAMIE   Actually that was hellish. I was desperate to get away. Maybe it's my age but it was driving me insane. All that noise . . . the drag queens and leather queens and dancing queens, and every bloody type of bloody queen you can imagine, it's too much. Everywhere you look there's rainbow flags, women with nails through their tits, fifty year old men with beards dressed as Judy Garland. At one point I thought I was going to be knocked off my feet by a bank of low flying formation Kylies. I looked around and thought I shouldn't be here. I don't fit in with these people – I'm not a prostitute or a fashion designer or someone from the menswear department of Selfridges. I live in Croydon for Christ's sake! I work in a bank! I'm not part of all this! You can't go putting a bolt through your penis if you live in South Croydon and work in the Alliance & Leicster! Where are the straight people? I just want to see someone wearing a Shell Suit, eating a Wimpy and playing Bingo before my head explodes! (*Pause.*) Are you alright in there?

(MARK *enters with wet hair and a towel, sits down with his coffee.*)

MARK   Yeah I'm OK. I'm a bit wet. Where shall I put this?

JAMIE   Just leave it on the side. Hang your trousers up to dry if you want.

MARK   You trying to get me out of 'em already?!

JAMIE   (*purposefully*) No. Not at all. I said you can come in and dry off and for a chat. (*Beat.*) But that is all, Mark. I'm serious. I just want to be your friend. We can be friends. It is possible. Nothing wrong with that. (*Little pause. Mood changes.*) What were you doing out there in the rain anyway?

MARK   Just walking past.

          (*Little pause.*)

JAMIE   You're soaked to the bone. You must have been out there for ages.

MARK   Nah.

(*Pause.* JAMIE *is slightly spooked.*)

JAMIE   Well, what were you doing?

          (*Awkward pause.*)

MARK   Shopping.

JAMIE   In South Croydon? (*Little pause as* JAMIE *thinks.*)
          What for – Asbos? I don't mean that. You haven't
          got any shopping.

MARK   Didn't see anything I liked.

JAMIE   Haven't you got an umbrella?

MARK   I don't feel the rain, really. Not really. I don't mind
          it.

          (*Little pause.*)

JAMIE   Well. Nothing gets to you. Drink your tea. It will
          get cold. (JAMIE *watches* MARK *drink, he ponders
          why he is here.*) I'll get you a dry T-shirt.

MARK   Thanks.

          (JAMIE *goes out and gets a T-shirt.* MARK *walks up
          to the framed picture of* NIGEL *and* JAMIE *on the
          shelf and looks at it. He hears* JAMIE *coming back
          in and puts it back down.*)

JAMIE   Here. This should fit you.

          (JAMIE *hands* MARK *a clean T-shirt.* MARK*s
          changes. Purposefully* JAMIE *takes holds the dry
          T-shirt out for him, and takes the wet one. He puts
          it out to dry. He holds up tracksuit bottoms.*)

JAMIE   I've got these, Trackie-B's.

          (MARK *nods and takes off his wet jeans.* JAMIE *is
          embarrassed and purposefully turns away so he*

doesn't look as MARK *changes. Again he holds out the dry tracksuit bottoms which* MARK *takes and puts the wet ones down which* JAMIE *takes.*)

JAMIE   Are you cold? Shall I turn the heating up?

MARK   It's OK. Thanks.

JAMIE   It's alright?

MARK   Yeah. (*Break in dialogue as* JAMIE *goes to the phone and dials 1471 and puts the phone down when he sees* NIGEL *hasn't called.*) Has he called?

JAMIE   No. He will do.

MARK   Sorry if I've ruined it.

JAMIE   What?

MARK   Your day.

JAMIE   How have you haven't ruined my day? I wasn't meant to be back here. It's not your fault. Glad to have the company really.

MARK   Don't you think you should call your boyfriend?

JAMIE   Why? He's not called me.

MARK   It's stupid to be rowing, innit.

JAMIE   Well I told you earlier, didn't I. Relationships aren't as easy or as straight forward as you might think they are, from the outside. The grass is always greener.

MARK   No. But there's no point in rowing. Good to be the first to say sorry.

JAMIE   Maybe. Not all the time though.

(*The phone rings.*)

MARK   Maybe that's him.

(JAMIE *looks. The answerphone comes on.*)

NIGEL   (*voice on answerphone*) Hi, this is Nigel and Jamie, we're not in at the moment but leave a message and we'll get back to you. Cheers.

VOICE   Hi honey, it's Alex. Are you there? . . . Jamie, will you pick up if you're there . . . I don't know what's gone on but I've just found Nigel pissed out of his head, said you had a row. I don't know if you're at home or if you've gone to Simba's or you're with Dave or Ellie or what but please give me a call and let me know you are OK because we are worried about you. I'll leave another message on your mobile, alright. Love you. Bye.

MARK   You should call them back.

JAMIE   I will, I'll send a text. I don't want to talk to anybody. Please take notice: it's not him calling. (*Little pause.*) You could still go to Pride though.

MARK   Nah.

JAMIE   I still say you'd enjoy it. Best time to, when you're young.

MARK   There's enough people there without you tying to bump up the numbers.

JAMIE   Actually that's not true any more. There used to be hundreds of thousands. They're lucky if they get forty or fifty now. The late nineties weren't particularly good for gay people.

MARK   Why's that? What happened? Aids?

JAMIE   No, Steps.

MARK   What?

JAMIE   It just got a bit commercial and naff and full of shit
         boy bands.

MARK   Fuck that.

JAMIE   The political thing is important though. Gay rights.
         Always march for Peter Tatchell or Stonewall. Ian
         McKellen, all that lot. (MARK *stares*.) Gandalf. You
         should look him up. (*Little pause.*) You might meet
         a boyfriend there.

MARK   I don't wanna meet any boyfriends. What's the
         point?

JAMIE   There's lots of point.

MARK   Why? It's not what I want – bumming around with
         every second bastard I see. I 'ate it. I don't wanna
         spend my whole life moving from one person to
         the next every time the music stops.

JAMIE   Well you don't have to do that. I'm sure there's
         someone out there for you.

MARK   Yeah, right.

         (*Little pause.*)

JAMIE   I'm sure. There is.

MARK   Don't matter even if I do meet someone. Gay
         people can't have proper relationships – not like
         normal people.

JAMIE   Mark, that's not true. Why do you say that? It's
         horrible that you say that.

MARK   They can't be faithful to each other.

JAMIE   You can if you want to. If that's what you choose.

MARK   No! Gays can't do it. Everyone knows it!

JAMIE   Who says that?

MARK   Everyone! Parents. School. Gay magazines.

JAMIE   Mark. That. Is. Not. True. Just because you
            haven't met the love of your life yet doesn't mean
            you won't tomorrow or the day after or next
            month, next year, ten years whenever. You don't
            realise how bloody young you are. And you're
            having fun, aren't you. What's wrong with that?
            For goodness sake, seventeen! When I was
            seventeen I could have been thrown in prison for
            doing what we did last night, I had to wait till I
            was twenty-one to do anything with anyone.

MARK   What's your point?

JAMIE   That you've got plenty of time left. There's no
            rush. You haven't begun. You'll have loads of
            nice boyfriends, give it time and then one day,
            you'll meet someone special.

MARK   What makes you so sure?

JAMIE   Because you will.

MARK   Why? You haven't.

JAMIE   Yes I have.

MARK   Oh right. Celebrating your anniversary on his own,
            is he?

            (JAMIE *gets up*.)

JAMIE   Probably.

MARK   I'm sorry.

JAMIE   No . . . probably not/

MARK   /No, I'm sorry, mate. I'm out of order.

JAMIE   Probably not on his own at all.

MARK   /It ain't my place to say . . .

JAMIE   /No, you're right!

MARK   /It's up to you what you do.

JAMIE   No, you are, you're right. Where is he? It's our
            tenth anniversary! I've called his phone and it's
            on voicemail. He told me to fuck off!

MARK   Maybe he'll be back any minute, maybe he'll call.

JAMIE   It's pathetic. Jesus Christ, you're counselling me.

MARK   It's still early.

JAMIE   No, thanks Mark but don't try and make me feel
            better, I don't need it. I know where he is. He's
            probably off with some guy somewhere, doing God
            knows what, I know what he's like.

            (*Little pause.*)

MARK   Can I ask you something?

JAMIE   Yes.

MARK   Why don't you leave him?

JAMIE   I don't want to leave him. (*Pause.*) We had a trial
            separation for a year in '97. He went round
            shagging everything that moved and wasn't
            pinned down. I met this guy and we started seeing
            each other. He was great – Gavin, he was called.
            Good looking, very kind, generous and great for
            me – everyone said it.

MARK   Why didn't you stay with him?

JAMIE   I would have done . . . but he died. (*Beat.*) The
            truth is . . . he couldn't handle being gay.

MARK   Oh my God, did he kill himself?

JAMIE   No, he burnt his nose on a bottle of poppers and fell down the stairs. (*Beat.*) It was awful. (*Pause.*) I'm joking. It just could never have worked out between us. He was boring. Yes he was nice to me but I just missed Nigel. To look at it you wouldn't know it but Nigel and I used to get on so well. We were this golden couple. We did everything together. He used to laugh at everything I'd say. I was the funny one and he was the big strong one, he'd look out for me. He used to be very protective with me.

MARK   Did he?

JAMIE   He got into a fight once. We were in the Southern Pride and some vile queen came up to me when Nigel was getting a drink. He said he really liked me, and was that my boyfriend. I said it was and he said he didn't care and could he have my number anyway. I mentioned it to Nigel and he went mad, shouting, the bloke shat himself. (*Beat.*) Sometimes we would just stay in our own at weekends, all weekend. Didn't need to be around other people. We'd have something to eat, a bottle of wine and just sit up talking. He'd sit up in bed with me, laughing. He'd put his big arms round me and I just felt – really stupid, it is – kind of, I can't believe I'm saying this – but kind of . . . safe, like I could let go of this façade of who I was with other people and just be myself. I could smell that smell of his and feel his hard body and the warmth of his breath going in and out, over me and I felt protected. (*Little pause.*) But we never talk any more. He doesn't laugh at my jokes, his eyes don't light up when he sees me, he just looks weary, bored. I get short tempered with him, I don't mean to but I do. He looks at other people all the time, then he talks to other people, then he sleeps with other people. I've just gotten used to it. What else can I do? I look at him sometimes and it's like looking a clock counting down and the time is running out and there's nothing that anyone can do to stop it. Do you know what I mean?

MARK   Like on Countdown?

          (JAMIE *stares at him.*)

JAMIE   No, not really. Worse than that.

MARK   Worse than that?

JAMIE   Yes, much worse.

MARK   Like Ready Steady Cook? Or Big Brother when
          you've got two minutes to leave the house? Or/

JAMIE   No, no let's forget that . . . (JAMIE *opens a can of
          beer.*) Just things have changed. We still laugh
          every now and then but not very often and it's not
          the same. Sometimes I think he's laughing with me,
          but I look again, it's just like things are on auto-
          pilot. Everything's there. On paper it's just how it
          used to be but it's just not the same – and you
          pretend it's like it used to be but really deep
          down, everyone knows it's not.

MARK   Like when Ainsley Harriot took over from Fern
          Britten?

JAMIE   Yes, like with Ainsley Harriot. That's right.
          Sometimes I think Nigel would much rather be with
          Fern Britten than me.

MARK   Well, he can't, she's got Philip Schofield now.

JAMIE   Yeah, alright, can we move on from the Daytime
          TV thing.

MARK   Sorry.

          (JAMIE *stares at him.*)

JAMIE   Thank you. (*Pause.*) Sometimes I see this look in
          his eyes. It's a look of sadness. Like he's
          wondering if he made a mistake, like he would
          much rather he was with someone else, or just
          anyone but with me, and I realise it, I can't

pretend to myself, like I do all the rest of the time, I can't dress it up, or make some joke and talk my way out of, it's there for me to see – he doesn't want me any more. This man that I have loved so hard and for so long, doesn't want me any more. (*Little pause.*) And it kills me.

(*Pause.*)

MARK   I would love you back. Just as much . . . if I was your boyfriend.

JAMIE   But you're not my boyfriend. You can't be.

MARK   Why not? People think I'm stupid 'cos I don't go on about myself all the time or say wanky things but I'm not. I'm working my way up to get where I wanna be. I'm gonna be a chef in a proper restaurant one day. I ain't got no one helping me but I'm doing it. And I want someone nice with me. I'm a romantic person. I hate Gaydar! That's not what I want. When I was little I thought one day I'll meet someone who'll take me out and woo me, take the time to find out what I'm into, what makes me tick. (*Beat.*) You go on Gaydar and all they wanna know is if you give it or take it, how big your cock is and if there's a tube stop near your house. (*Little pause.*) And I hate that!

JAMIE   Because it's so shallow?

MARK   No, 'cos Croydon's not on the tube! You can tell them to get on the tram but it's not the same! (*Beat.*) Yes, 'cos it's shallow! (*Little pause.*) I want something more than all this. I know you could give it to me.

JAMIE   We don't know each other.

MARK   That doesn't matter. You feel it too. Something special. I knew it when I saw you – that you're the kind of man I could be boyfriends with. And love and be faithful to and stay with forever. I mean it.

That's all I want, too. Like you. Come back with me, to mine tonight.

JAMIE   Just like that? Just walk out.

MARK   Just leave him a note.

JAMIE   I can't do that, Mark.

MARK   Well, let's get out of here then. I don't want to be here where he could walk in at any minute. Come back with me, come and spend some time at mine and if you want you can come back here and tell him tomorrow or whenever . . . you keep telling me about gay pride, that I can meet a boyfriend and be happy and be just as happy as straight people. Well prove it. Prove it to me. Leave him. Leave him and I'll believe in everything you're telling me about being proud and finding a boyfriend and how everything can be for me. If you can't find what you want in life then how am I supposed to believe that I can? So tomorrow. Come back with me now. And then tell him that you're leaving him.

          (*Pause.*)

JAMIE   Are you out of your mind?

MARK   What have you got to lose? (*Little pause.*) It's time to move on from Nigel. Time to put yourself first for once, Jamie. It's time to put your money where your mouth is. You've already broken one of the rules. You're breaking another one right now. (*They kiss.*) It's time you broke number three, four and all the rest of 'em.

          (*Blackout.*)

ACT TWO

Scene One

We hear rain. Stan by Eminem plays.

JAMIE *and* NIGEL'S *flat. 6.10 am Sunday morning. The sun is starting to rise. There is a flickering light from the TV. Trisha is on at a low but audible volume. As the scene unfolds the sun should slowly be rising and the light increases.*

JAMIE *is slumped on the sofa, smoking. There is a suitcase packed in a corner. We hear* NIGEL *putting his key in the lock.* JAMIE *looks up expectantly looking to see* NIGEL *come in. He doesn't. There is a prolonged silence and sound of a door banging open.*

NIGEL   (*off*) Fuck it!

            (NIGEL *staggers in, still high or drunk, and doesn't notice* JAMIE *at first. He puts down his bag. He is chewing gum and has a take out bag from Balans cafe. He sees* JAMIE.)

            Jesus, why are you sitting in the dark? It's ten past six. Why are you still up? (*Pause.* NIGEL *sighs.*) Oh, take off my shoes, will you. (JAMIE *stares.* NIGEL *giggles sheepishly.*) They wouldn't take my bag at the cloakroom at Fire so I had to stand with it on the dancefloor. It was a nightmare with all these dumb Muscle Marys dancing round me, kicking it the whole time. (*Little pause.*) Jamie? (JAMIE *looks up and acknowledges him for the first time.*) You OK?

JAMIE   I'm fine.

NIGEL   I got you a present.

JAMIE   Did you?

NIGEL   Look. (*He turns the light on.*) Breakfast from
Balans. I've got you a smoked salmon bagel with
cream cheese – low fat, and a piece of carrot cake.

JAMIE   Thank you, that's kind of you, you didn't have to.

NIGEL   I know I didn't have to but I wanted to. I like
doing things for my lovely boyfriend. Don't I? We
went up there for a coffee afterwards. Do you want
it now?

JAMIE   No, in the morning.

NIGEL   Have it now.

JAMIE   (*firmly*) I'll have it later.

        (*Beat.*)

NIGEL   Oh. OK. (*Beat.*) You sure you're alright?

JAMIE   Yes.

NIGEL   Good. Why don't we go out tomorrow night, for
that dinner we talked about? Anniversary treat. J
Sheekey's. You can get the lobster, I'll pay.
(JAMIE *nods.*) Great. We can call lovely Ben, he can
get us in there. (*Pause.*) What did you do last
night?

JAMIE   What do you think I did?

        (*He turns the TV off.*)

NIGEL   Did you go to G.A.Y.? Was Dannii good?

JAMIE   No I didn't do much at all apart from wait for you.
(*Pause.*) Went for a walk around town then came
back here and not much really, nothing important
. . . I don't think. I got a Chinese. Watched a
video. Spoke to Laura on the phone.

NIGEL   Oh right. How's she? Everything alright?

JAMIE   No, not really. I think they're going to split up.

NIGEL   Really?

JAMIE   She's thinking about leaving. That's what she's saying.

NIGEL   I'll believe that when I see it. The only way they'd ever split up is if he walked out.

JAMIE   You don't think she'd ever have the guts to go?

NIGEL   Do you seriously think she would? Can you imagine it? She wouldn't know what to do without him. It'd be like having a leg cut off.

JAMIE   Maybe.

NIGEL   She's a doormat. Always been the same since I've known her.

JAMIE   Well you know sometimes people do things you don't expect them to. And actually people do find her attractive, hard as it may be for you to believe. Might take a while but I'm sure she would meet someone else.

NIGEL   You reckon. Maybe if she hangs around Chessington Zoo long enough. Not going to happen is it, let's be honest. She won't leave.

JAMIE   Well maybe you're right. Who knows.

NIGEL   What else did you do?

JAMIE   Nothing. I've just been sitting up waiting for you.

NIGEL   Why didn't you go to bed?

(*Little pause.*)

JAMIE   Just wanted to make sure you got home OK. (*Pause.*) Late. Isn't it? (*Beat.*) How are you, anyway?

NIGEL   Fucked, to be honest.

JAMIE   Do you want some water? (*Holds up his bottle of Evian.*)

NIGEL   Got this.

JAMIE   What did you take?

NIGEL   Not much. Couple of pills, some coke.

JAMIE   Do you want some juice?

NIGEL   That'd be good.

         (JAMIE *gets up and goes to the kitchen and pours* NIGEL *a glass of orange juice,* NIGEL *switches on the PC and goes about logging into Gaydar.*)

NIGEL   Oh, my God, it was am amazing night. Orange was rammed to the rafters. Ross ended up in the toilets with these two guys. Really cute they were. One was some Brazilian queen on holiday, the other was a model. Or so he said. You know what these lying twats are like. He was gorgeous, mind you. Scottish. Three of them all packed into a cubicle. Even I thought that was outrageous. The toilets there are so small for one thing. (JAMIE *comes in with the glass and a carton of orange juice.*) Can you believe it?

JAMIE   (*shaking his head to himself*) Yes I can . . . Where's your jacket?

NIGEL   You what?

JAMIE   Your jacket. You had it when you went out.

         (NIGEL *looks round at his things.*)

NIGEL   Oh yeah, fuck it.

JAMIE   You lost it?

NIGEL   No, I left it with Paul and Amyn in Balans. They sent me a text just after I left. Said I'd get it tomorrow. That's alright isn't it.

JAMIE   Of course.

NIGEL   God, I am so horny, aren't you? (*He taps his
               password into the computer.*) Fucking hell.

               (*Little pause.*)

JAMIE   No messages?

NIGEL   No. Damn. I wonder if the boys of south London
               are still up. I bet they're all down the Fridge in
               that backroom, the dirty little buggers. (*Pause.*)
               One hundred and twenty five people in south
               London cruising. At six in the morning. Now are
               they awake, have they just got in or are they just
               leaving the hook dangling while they're asleep.
               'ADSL, may not be at computer.' That annoys me.
               Fucking selfish aren't they, people. You don't
               know who've got a chance with because 'cos you
               don't know who's really there? We got any
               vodka?

JAMIE   There's a new one in there.

               (*He gets up, kisses* JAMIE *on the head and goes to
               the kitchen.*)

NIGEL   D'you want one?

JAMIE   Thanks. (*Little pause.*) So, I didn't get any
               messages either.

NIGEL   Say again?

JAMIE   I didn't get any messages tonight.

NIGEL   From who?

JAMIE   From Ben Affleck. From you. I didn't get any
               messages from you.

NIGEL   Sorry. I didn't get a chance.

JAMIE   You didn't have two seconds where you could
         have turned your phone on and sent a text?

NIGEL   You knew I'd be out with Ross, and Ickle and
         Gianluca and the boys.

JAMIE   You could have been lying dead in a gutter for all I
         knew.

NIGEL   Awwww Jamesey. That's sweet. I'm sorry. I didn't
         mean to worry you. I was off my head. (*He has
         come back in with the vodka bottle and two
         glasses full of ice.*) Sorry. (*He kisses* JAMIE *on the
         head and sits down in front of the PC.*)

JAMIE   I'm sorry too for rowing.

NIGEL   Don't be silly it's fine, I forgive you. Hold your
         glass up.

         (NIGEL *pours him a drink.*)

JAMIE   OK. I didn't mean to freak out.

         (NIGEL *pours them both drinks.*)

NIGEL   Whatever. I've forgotten it.

JAMIE   I shouldn't have done that. I shouldn't have gone.

NIGEL   Look, you were in a bad mood, you didn't want to
         be there so you went home. I wish you'd stayed, I
         didn't want you to go but fair enough. The guys
         were there, Ross was there . . . I was fine. I had a
         nice time.

JAMIE   Did you? Good. That's good. (*Pause.*) Shall we go
         to bed? I'm very tired.

NIGEL   In a minute. Just see who's on.

JAMIE   OK. (*Pause.*) I should tidy up I s'pose.

NIGEL   You've made a bloody mess. Looks like you've
             had your own gay pride in here.

             (JAMIE *gets up and takes a few plates out and
             empty carton of Chinese food.* NIGEL *attends to
             Gaydar.*)

JAMIE   What was the rest of the day like?

NIGEL   Really good. Compton Street was heaving, they
             shut it all off. It was fun, it really worked.

JAMIE   Good.

             (*We hear the noise of a message arriving.*)

NIGEL   That Carlhot bloke from Elephant and Castle. Oh
             God, I love him. 'Sorry mate, you're too old. I'm
             not being funny but I have told you before, I'm
             not interested. Happy hunting though'. What an
             arrogant little shit. I saw him out tonight going
             into Vauxhall tube. He was on his own then.
             Probably still can't find anyone but oh no, we're
             too old, he's still too good for us. Picky fucker.
             Should have gone over and clubbed him over the
             head. I will do next time. (*Laughs.*) He's nice.

             (NIGEL *types into keyboard.*)

JAMIE   What happened with that guy?

NIGEL   What guy?

JAMIE   The one you were snogging on the march.

NIGEL   Snogging? Who was I snogging on the march?
             (*Beat.*) Oh him, when you left? Nothing. Who
             knows where he went, he disappeared, silly arse. I
             told you it was nothing. I'm not going to actually
             do anything at Pride am I. You silly boy; over-
             reacting.

JAMIE   Yes. (*Beat.*) Didn't the rain spoil it?

NIGEL Everyone just piled into the bars. Then it stopped, everyone came out again. Fun. I missed my Westlife but what can you do.

JAMIE (*smiling*) You missed Westlife? They're not something you'd miss exactly are they?

NIGEL They're good.

JAMIE There's more interesting things to do at Pride than watching some dumb boy-band monkeys, don't you think?

NIGEL I missed them.

JAMIE I wouldn't miss them. I'd make sure I aimed properly.

NIGEL Ha.

JAMIE Actually I was glad I left. I wasn't really feeling it today.

NIGEL What do you mean you weren't feeling it?

JAMIE Maybe I'm starting to grow out of it.

NIGEL It's a party, you don't grow out of a party.

JAMIE It just seemed a bit strange today. I don't think I get much of a thrill any more from being surrounded by a bunch of drag queens and E'd up bitchy kids in their underwear. (*Beat.*) Actually maybe that's not fair. I just wasn't in the right mood to appreciate it. Ruined the day a bit, didn't I. (*Little pause.*) Floats looked nice. (*Little pause.*) Come on – bed.

NIGEL Not yet.

(*Little pause.*)

JAMIE   Come on, it's so late. Early. We could go into
             town tomorrow. Go to the park. Feed the ducks,
             maybe. Before we go for food.

NIGEL   OK, I'll shut it down. (*Sound of a message as*
             NIGEL *receives another one.*) Ah. He's nice. Look
             at him. Wants a blow job. Oooh, you never know.
             Where is he? Camberwell. (*Types into computer.*)
             Accommodate or travel?

JAMIE   What? Are you going to go out?

NIGEL   Could do.

JAMIE   Are you serious?

NIGEL   It's not far. Twenty minutes this time of night.

JAMIE   You can't drive, you're out of it.

NIGEL   Hmm. No one will be around.

JAMIE   No. I'm not letting you drive.

             (*Little pause.*)

NIGEL   We can get a cab. Yeah, do that.

JAMIE   I don't want to. I'm tired. I want to go to bed.
             Come on, it's still our weekend, let's have one
             night together while we can.

             (*Little pause.*)

NIGEL   Look – Dick size: large.

JAMIE   I don't care.

NIGEL   I do. You just need one more drink.

JAMIE   No. (NIGEL *pours himself one.*) I need bed.

NIGEL   Has he sent one back?

JAMIE   And you do, too.

NIGEL   Come on, come on, come on . . . /

JAMIE   /We can do something nice tomorrow if we get up
         early enough.

NIGEL   You are being *silly.* You need to relax. It's still
         Pride weekend. I'll pour you one.

         (*He pours* JAMIE *a drink.*)

JAMIE   Well you go if you want. I'm not.

NIGEL   Do you mind? (*A new message arrives.*) Yes! He's
         up for it.

         (NIGEL *gets up and goes to the bedroom.*)

JAMIE   Yes I do mind. What are you doing?

NIGEL   I stink.

         (*He comes back in with a deodorant and a T-
         shirt. He changes T-shirt and sprays on some
         deodorant.*)

JAMIE   You are seriously going out now?

NIGEL   (*puts his arm round him, hands him a glass with
         ice and vodka in it which he pushes back*) Yeah,
         come with. Come on. You'll enjoy it. You just need
         to have a drink, you're uptight, I can tell.

JAMIE   (*emphasising*) Nigel, no. I don't want another
         drink.

NIGEL   It'll get you in the mood. And I've got poppers.

JAMIE   Why? Why have you got poppers?

NIGEL   Just have.

JAMIE   When did you get them?

NIGEL   Earlier.

JAMIE   What for?

            (*Beat.*)

NIGEL   Dancing. Look at him, that private one.

JAMIE   (*getting up*) Jesus.

NIGEL   One drinkie.

JAMIE   Look, I'm not going to bed and I'm not going out.
            We need to talk.

NIGEL   Jamie needs a drink!

JAMIE   Leave it will you . . .

NIGEL   Have a vodka.

JAMIE   I don't want a vodka . . .

NIGEL   A voddie voddie vodka!

JAMIE   No!

NIGEL   Take the drink, you know you want to. Go on/

            (NIGEL *forces the drink into* JAMIE'S *hands as he's
            pouring it.*)

JAMIE   (*screaming*) Look, I don't want a fucking drink,
            alright! And turn this piece of shit off!

            (*He pushes* NIGEL *away and* NIGEL *drops the
            bottle and the glass on the floor.*)

NIGEL   Jesus Christ, what's the matter with you?

JAMIE   Will you shut the fuck up and listen to me for
            once?!

(*Pause.*)

NIGEL   Who's going to clean this up?! I'm not doing it.

JAMIE   I don't give a damn who cleans it up! (*Pause.*)
Nigel. We. Need. To talk.

(*A message comes through.*)

NIGEL   It's Camberwell.

JAMIE   (*screaming*) Fuck him!

NIGEL   Alright!

JAMIE   What's wrong with you!? You're obsessed.

NIGEL   I've stopped it.

JAMIE   We can't have a conversation without you having
that thing on. I wish we'd never bought that
fucking computer!

NIGEL   OK. I'm not doing it now. What do you want to
talk about?

(*Pause.* JAMIE *paces up and down.*)

JAMIE   Things.

NIGEL   Well! I'm listening!

JAMIE   Your attitude . . . (*Beat.*) to things . . .

NIGEL   Yes?

JAMIE   . . . is pissing me off. It's getting on top of me. It's
getting on my nerves.

NIGEL   What is?

JAMIE   I don't know. Lots of things.

NIGEL   Tell me if I've done something.

JAMIE   You have.

NIGEL   Like what?

JAMIE   Well . . . yesterday for instance, Friday. With that
            boy.

NIGEL   That boy?

JAMIE   That boy who came round on Friday night.

NIGEL   What about him?

JAMIE   It embarrassed me.

NIGEL   What do you feel embarrassed about? OK we lied
            about our ages, he didn't mind or know. Do you
            mean your stomach? It isn't washboard any more
            but it doesn't matter. The lights were out, he
            wouldn't have noticed.

JAMIE   I don't mean that! I felt embarrassed that we had
            him round here at all. Seventeen!

NIGEL   Oh, please.

JAMIE   And we were drooling over him like a pair of
            perverts . . .

NIGEL   That's what he wanted.

JAMIE   Maybe so.

NIGEL   What do you *think* he was online for?

JAMIE   That doesn't make it right. He didn't need a shag,
            he needed someone to talk to. Maybe we should
            have said no. Maybe we should have sent him
            home.

NIGEL   Sent him home? Don't be so stupid.

JAMIE   It didn't feel right to me.

NIGEL	What's their to feel right about? It's fucking. It felt right to me.
JAMIE	Obviously. (*Little pause.*) I don't want to do that any more.
NIGEL	Fine, don't then. No one's forcing you.
JAMIE	Aren't they? Feels like it.
NIGEL	What's that supposed to mean? You don't have to do anything you don't want to. We both decided to have an open relationship.
JAMIE	We don't have an open relationship!
NIGEL	To have threesomes then, you know what I mean.
JAMIE	That was years ago.
NIGEL	Well you've not brought it up. You can change your mind at any time.
JAMIE	Oh really.
NIGEL	Yes, really.
JAMIE	Well I tried to change it today and look at the way you reacted.
NIGEL	(*still relatively good humoured*) Well it's not the time, is it – when I'm on someone's face.
JAMIE	Hmm.
NIGEL	And you overreacted. You threw a fit over nothing.
JAMIE	It was not a fit. I tried to pull you away. I said I didn't like it. I didn't like it, so I said so.
NIGEL	It was a tantrum! Now that was embarrassing – in front of all those people. You're not eight years

old you know! Yes, I might have gone too far but why should I have the day ruined because my boyfriend's being an attention seeking little twat?

JAMIE   It's our tenth anniversary!

NIGEL   You keep saying that. And what?!

JAMIE   Sorry if I get upset that you're getting off with someone. It's meant to mean that you put me first. Not strangers and drag acts.

NIGEL   It's Pride. That's what it's about. I like Pride. Up until today, I always thought you did, too.

JAMIE   Who knows any more. Maybe I pretended for the last few years because I know how much you love it and look forward to it, like I pretend about a lot of things these days . . . I used to go because it felt like there was actually some meaning to it; some politics, heaven forbid! Huh! The final gay taboo – having your own point of view!

NIGEL   Here we go again, with your Peter Tatchell bullshit.

JAMIE   What's he got to do with it?

NIGEL   That fucking loon. (*Beat.*) You want to know the reason why people really get queerbashed? People see him banner waving, that nutcase, zealot and it gives us all a bad name. And people like you support him! Tell me who died and made that man gay King? Who gave him the right to speak for everybody?

JAMIE   He doesn't claim to speak for anyone . . . /

NIGEL   He doesn't speak for me, I'll tell you that. He just upsets everyone. It's counterproductive. Instead of pissing around squealing at everybody, what he should be doing is/

JAMIE What do you mean what he 'should be doing'? You 'should be doing', I 'should be doing', we 'should' all 'be doing' but we're not, are we. Fine. But don't start having a go at somebody who actually gets off his arse and does something. It's a miracle that someone inspired you to fill out a Stonewall postcard once in the last decade. Who do you think you are? (*Beat.*) Jesus Christ!

(*Pause.* NIGEL *becomes calmer and more serious.*)

NIGEL (*quietly*) What do you mean you pretend?

JAMIE What?

NIGEL You said you pretend about a lot of things these days? (*Little pause.*) What do you mean by that Jamie?

JAMIE (*slowly and quietly*) I've got something to . . . (*Beat.*) I think I've made a decision, Nige . . .

NIGEL A decision about what?

JAMIE (*slowly*) I think I've realised that . . .

(*Beat.*)

NIGEL What?

JAMIE I'm not happy any more.

(*Pause.*)

NIGEL With me?

JAMIE With all of it.

NIGEL I don't understand. You don't have to go to Pride if you don't want to. You didn't. You left. I didn't stop you, did I?

JAMIE No. (*Beat.*) *You* didn't stop me, did you.

(*Pause.*)

NIGEL   That was because it was/

JAMIE   Oh Nigel, it's not just about Pride. If you enjoy it, then great. I normally have a laugh when I get there, it's just one day. It's the other 364 that worry me.

NIGEL   What are you talking about?

JAMIE   I'm thirty. You're thirty-two and all we do is go out dancing, get pissed, get high on pills every weekend and look for people to sleep with. It's all we ever do, it's our life and I don't think I want that any more.

NIGEL   You make it sound like all we ever do is have sex.

JAMIE   Well it is, isn't it?

NIGEL   No it isn't. We do lots of things.

(*Little pause.*)

JAMIE   Like what?

NIGEL   What do you mean like what? We do loads of things – we go shopping, go to the gym . . .

JAMIE   Oh ha, the first thing you mention would be the gym wouldn't it.

NIGEL   What's wrong with the gym?

JAMIE   Nothing wrong with it. There's just something about the way you say it. 'The gym, the gym'. Like it's just a word, like it isn't loaded, like it isn't the most important box ticked as part of the whole lifestyle package you've signed up to.

NIGEL   What's wrong with keeping yourself fit?

JAMIE   Nothing but that isn't why you go is it. What are *you* gonna get – repetitive strain injury of the eye? I don't know why you bother getting the full membership, you should just go in and ask for 'One to view'.

NIGEL   There's naked bodies, you're gonna look, so what! What a hypocrite you are – you're all for reading books and improving your mind, just because some people want to improve their bodies you go mad. Better mind, we like. Better body, you're shallow, you're fucked up.

JAMIE   I'm not saying that and it's not the same.

NIGEL   Yes it is.

JAMIE   No it isn't. I don't see people parading their minds down spunk alley in Vauxhall.

NIGEL   If I go to the gym and I want a better body it's for me, it makes me feel better. And for you for that matter.

JAMIE   For me? Thank you.

NIGEL   You're welcome.

JAMIE   You don't do it for me. You don't need to attract me, I'm stuck here, like an Oak tree planted in the ground with roots so deep you know you can't pull out. It's the rest of them you want buzzing round you like you're a neon light in a kebab shop.

NIGEL   You're stuck here are you? Great.

JAMIE   I don't mean that, I don't know what I mean.

NIGEL   Tell me something I don't know. (*More annoyed.*) You have a good life with me. We go out all the time – we go to the theatre.

JAMIE   Only when you've read in QX that it's a play
         where they get their arses out. Or when it says on
         the posters 'Warning: this play contains nudity'.

NIGEL   Your problem is that you have always been one of
         those pathetic little queers that's wants to be
         straight. And if you can't be straight then you do
         the next best thing and spend your whole life
         worrying about what they think of us. Don't hold
         hands, someone will see, don't give me a kiss
         goodbye, because there might be someone with
         kids looking.

JAMIE   I have never said that!

NIGEL   It's boring, Jamie.

JAMIE   I don't give a fuck what straight people think. It's
         not up to them to judge what is right and wrong.
         But what I do care about is what I think.

NIGEL   And what's wrong with Gaydar? I have made
         friends on there. Lots of them.

JAMIE   Oh yeah, you're always on there looking for
         friends aren't you. At 2.00 am. Hello, I've got the
         sherry out, come over now and make friends. Be
         honest, Nige!

NIGEL   I have made friends off of Gaydar.

JAMIE   Like who? That woman at the clap clinic?

NIGEL   Very fucking funny. What's Sue got to do with it?
         I've had a few chats with her, I hardly know her.

JAMIE   She's asked you to be Godfather to her daughter!

NIGEL   So we get on. Big deal. You are a hypocrite. You
         don't seem to mind Gaydar so much. You always
         seem keen enough when we're round at
         someone's. You always get a mouthful. You never
         complain.

JAMIE   What do you want me to say – I'm some kind of
         virgin, or that I'm going to be celibate, I'm not! I
         like sex but you know what? I am started to
         become bored with it now. I'm bored. I'm
         becoming desensitised to it all. (*He picks up a
         magazine off of the coffee table.*) Look at this! Piss
         night, cum night, scally night, rubber night, dress
         in football drag night . . . What is it now – every
         other club is about sex? The gay clubs are
         banging! God, that's true. I remember in the
         eighties when Aids first hit when some police
         chief in Manchester said that 'gays were
         swimming around in a cess pit of their own
         making'. Do you remember that? Everyone went
         mad. If someone said that now, all we'd wanna
         know was where the venue was and how much it
         was to get in with a flier! (*Little pause.*) And let's
         not forget everybody's favourite – pages and
         pages of whores. Where does it end? Why do you
         make me feel like I'm frigid because I don't want to
         immerse myself in this stuff all the time? The
         choice can't just be between being a saint or a
         slut. There must be a happy medium somewhere?

NIGEL   Yes. Don't go to the clubs and don't read the
         magazines.

JAMIE   I don't. Because I don't have to, I've got a whole
         life and friends and other things to do. But look at
         Cumboy17 . . . oh God I'm not calling him that,
         Mark, his name is Mark. Look at him/

NIGEL   I'll say/

JAMIE   – he's seventeen, he's finding his feet. Trying to
         find out who he is, where he fits in . . ./

NIGEL   /Uh, the poor little flower.

JAMIE   And there's only one place where people have any
         interest in him fitting in isn't there?

NIGEL   Oh fuck off/

JAMIE   Do you really think it's healthy – do you think it's good that he's going to grow up thinking the pinnacle of achievement is becoming a rent boy or a porn star? Do you?

NIGEL   It's up to people, what they do. Individuals.

JAMIE   You're the one who hates gays if you think he should aspire to being a product on sale in a shop window. I'm sorry, you can say what you want, but it is so fucked up.

NIGEL   It's not my fault if someone's good looking and people want them. Market forces. Supply and demand. You did economics at school.

JAMIE   Oh great, the civilised world, 2005 and it's still survival of the fittest is it?

NIGEL   I'm nice to people. I don't judge them on appearances, I treat people the way I expect to be treated no matter what they look like.

JAMIE   The way we talk about people is disgusting. Friday – chav, common, council. He's a human being.

NIGEL   (*getting angrier*) Sorry if I've got a bit of class, Bob-Fucking-Gay-Geldof. Are you trying to change the world, are you? You better start running because there's a long way to go. You know you are really getting on my tits now . . .

JAMIE   Well me and the rest of London!

NIGEL   If you don't like it, you know where you can go!

JAMIE   Maybe I will – I'm definitely making some changes.

NIGEL   I would love you to hear yourself, how sanctimonious you sound.

JAMIE   I will sound like what I like!/

Nigel   (*shouting, angry*) How dare you throw this shit at me!/

Jamie   . . . and I'll do what I want!/

Nigel   We took months to decide how to set the rules in this relationship!/

Jamie   . . . and what was the point?/

Nigel   I never did anything without you!/

Jamie   When it suited you . . ./

Nigel   We made every decision together!/

Jamie   Listen to you . . ./

Nigel   We did everything together!/

Jamie   . . . as if I'm supposed to be grateful . . ./

Nigel   We talk everything through before we do anything in this relationship!/

Jamie   . . . that is what you're saying after all . . .

Nigel   Ten years . . .

Jamie   (*shouting*) . . . isn't it?!

Nigel   Ten years of me always putting you before myself!

Jamie   . . . lucky fucking me, eh?

Nigel   And now you're trying to blame me . . ./

Jamie   It feels like a lifetime . . ./

Nigel   . . . for everything that's ever gone wrong! Just because you can't hack it in the grown up world. You can't trundle on for years saying you want

one thing and when you get bored of it, blame me
for the fact we did it in the first place!

JAMIE   Why can't I?

NIGEL   (*screaming*) Because it's called wanting to have
your cock and eat it!

JAMIE   You're such a snob but you don't like it when
anyone criticises you. Well you can't give it
unless you can take it! Isn't that what you always
told me, 'Big Boy'!?

NIGEL   I don't want to listen to your shit any more!

JAMIE   (*shouting*) Well don't tell me what I can and
cannot do!

NIGEL   (*shouting back*) Well make up your mind what you
want!

JAMIE   I have!

        (*Beat.*)

NIGEL   You're a schizophrenic! This has come out of the
fucking blue.

JAMIE   No, it hasn't!

NIGEL   Well, where has it come from then?!

JAMIE   It's been lots of things.

NIGEL   (*screams*) Like what?!

        (*Considered, unrushed pause. Tone changes
        completely.* JAMIE *pauses, then begins slowly and
        quietly, getting emotional during speech.*)

JAMIE   Well . . . (JAMIE *calms himself, shaking, gathers
        his thoughts.*) A couple of weeks ago we were with
        that guy from Wallington. By the station. We were
        in bed with him and I stopped for a minute to get a

glass of water, I don't know if you remember but I
did. I came back in and I was just looking at you –
with him.

NIGEL   Looking at me?

JAMIE   Looking at you, at your body. It was a turn on at
first like it's meant to be according to the
magazines. Then I was looking at your skin, the
smoothness and it reminded me of the first time I
ever saw you. I remembered what that was like.
How excited I was. How thrilled I was when you
asked me out and the first time we slept together.
How beautiful you were. Someone could have
given me gold or diamonds or all the money in the
fucking world and I wouldn't have swapped it for
you. There would be times when we would have
sex and you'd be on top of me, and we'd be naked
and hot, and you'd be kissing me and the sweat
would drip off of your face onto mine and I looked
into your eyes and it was like I could see God
looking back at me and through me and back out at
you. I knew it was love. I knew I had it. That thing
that everyone talks about, I'd found it with you
and I knew it could never get any better than that.
(*Pause.*) And then, last week I look at some dirty,
desperate, old pig hammering away on top of you,
treating you like a piece of meat, just using you as
something to wank into and I wanted to kill him.
(*Getting more angry, panicked.*) I wanted to
scream and drag him off you and say 'what the
fuck do you think you are doing? This is the most
precious person in the world, leave him alone, get
the fuck away from him!' (*Beat.*) But then I looked
at you and I saw the look in your face and you
were loving it and I remembered where we were
and what we were doing and that's what we'd
chosen to do. We'd chosen. To be there. With
him. (*Pause.*) You're not into me any more. You
can barely get off unless there's someone else
there, or we're watching porn.

NIGEL   That's not true. I do still fancy you.

JAMIE   (*mocking*) You fancy me, you fancy me. It's
            alright – I'm a grown up, you can be honest, I can
            take it.

NIGEL   I do!

JAMIE   Nigel, the last time we had sex, you had a wank
            while I held our Gary Lucy calendar up over my
            face.

NIGEL   It was just something different! I do fancy you. So
            we tart things up a bit sometimes? We've been
            together for ten years. Do you understand what
            that means? It changes things. It's never going to
            be the first fragile flushes of new love forever, is
            it? I always come back to you. We have the rules.

JAMIE   Oh the rules, the rules, the rules . . . what's the
            point? You don't stick to them. Who's kidding
            who? This is my rule. I don't want to live with
            someone who can only get themself off by
            thinking about having sex with other men. If it
            works for Liza Minelli then great. But it doesn't
            work for me. Not any more.

NIGEL   Well Paul and Barry are happy. They've been
            together for fifteen years and they're the best
            couple we know.

JAMIE   You're not understanding what I'm saying are
            you? I'm not saying open relationships are wrong.
            It's what Paul and Barry want and it works for
            them. But it's not what I want any more and I'm
            not going to pretend it is. Why should I?

NIGEL   So it's you, you, you, you, you. And I can just go
            fucking jump, can I? It doesn't matter about what I
            think we should do.

JAMIE   Of course it does. I know that's what you want
            and I respect it. I do. (*Beat.*) That's why I think we
            should call it a day. I'm nearly packed.

            (*He walks over to the hallway.*)

NIGEL   You what? Are you serious?

JAMIE   What else can we do?

NIGEL   After ten years?

         (JAMIE *goes to the door.*)

JAMIE   Have you got any better ideas?

NIGEL   Have you packed your bag?

JAMIE   I can come back for the rest.

NIGEL   You're going now? Don't be so stupid, you are
         such a fucking drama queen.

JAMIE   Well if I'm going I'm going. I'm not going to have
         one of those long, drawn out dramas that we seem
         to live on these days.

NIGEL   But I love you.

JAMIE   No, you love fucking around, you can't stop
         yourself.

NIGEL   I won't sleep with anyone else, then. I won't, we
         won't!

JAMIE   You'd give them up, all of them?

NIGEL   Yes!

JAMIE   Like you would. As if you could.

NIGEL   If it meant keeping us together I'd never go with
         anyone else again.

JAMIE   Do you know what you're saying? What that
         would take?

NIGEL   Yes. I do. Look, I'll get rid of my Gaydar profile,
         I'll shut it down. I'll do it now.

*(He goes to the computer and starts shutting it
down.)*

JAMIE   Are you sure? That's what it says on the screen –
            are you sure you want to remove your profile?
            Well, are you?

NIGEL   If you want me to.

JAMIE   Why bother? We both know you can create a new
            one behind my back. It will always be there, no
            matter how many profiles you delete. This isn't
            about Gaydar, it's about the truth. I think you've
            forgotten what it is. You've even been lying to me
            tonight.

NIGEL   What have I lied about tonight?

JAMIE   Those two guys in the toilet at Orange. They
            weren't with Ross at all, were they? They were
            with you.

NIGEL   No! They were with Ross!

JAMIE   Nigel, that's bullshit, it was you!

NIGEL   It was Ross, I swear!

JAMIE   I know that guilty look. I know what you're like.
            That's where you left your jacket, isn't it?

NIGEL   No!

JAMIE   You left it on the floor of some bog while you were
            chowing down on two blokes.

NIGEL   No, I told you, I left it at Balans and probably
            David and Dylan have got it, or Paul and Amyn
            and I'm going to get it back tomorrow.

JAMIE   That'll be a good one to see. What are you going
            to do – go and knock on the door of Fire, see if
            they've got it or say Ickle has lost it? What will it

be? Who do you think I am? This is me! I know you!

NIGEL   Call Ross! Call him now, if you don't believe me. He'll tell you it was him! Go on pick up the phone – right now!

JAMIE   He's lied for you before. He always does.

NIGEL   He's got no reason to lie for me now, he doesn't have to. Call him!

JAMIE   And humiliate myself even more? Oh, please tell me what my boyfriend was doing, Ross. No thanks! Look, I do not care that you did it, I just care that you can be big enough to tell me the truth. How can you have an open relationship or any relationship without trust. This is what this is all about. Admit it and it won't bother me. It won't. Tell me the truth, that you had sex with someone and we'll move on. Be honest and I will be honest too.

NIGEL   This is what it's about – sex, isn't it? Because you don't get as much as I do, it makes you bitter and you don't like it, because people want me. Because it's me that pulls them in.

JAMIE   Oh I knew it. Knew this would come up. So what are you saying? I'm not attractive? Is that it?

NIGEL   I'm not saying that.

JAMIE   You're implying it.

NIGEL   It's not my fault if they gravitate towards me, as they tend to do. I can't help the way I look.

JAMIE   Oh, the truth at last.

NIGEL   You said it, not me.

JAMIE   Am I not good enough for you any more?

NIGEL   Didn't say that/

JAMIE   Not hot enough, not toned enough . . . ?

NIGEL   If you feel you have problems meeting people it's
            probably because you're shy, that's all I think.

JAMIE   Ahh, we're down to the meat of it now . . . Mr
            fucking perfect.

NIGEL   It's your issues, not mine. You're perfectly good
            enough for me. Not my fault if you don't feel you
            are. Yeah I get more attention, I don't think it
            makes me better than anyone else. What am I
            meant to do – give it up? To make you feel better
            about yourself?

JAMIE   I am attractive.

NIGEL   It's not my fault is it?

JAMIE   I do meet people. (*Little pause.*) I did. Today.

NIGEL   What?

JAMIE   You heard me.

NIGEL   What are you talking about?

JAMIE   We can have an amnesty, wipe the slate clean. Tell
            me the truth and I'll tell you the truth, too. And if
            you can't, I will call a cab and go and stay at the
            hotel up the road, I'll be back tomorrow to get the
            rest of my stuff and that will be it. And I mean
            that.

NIGEL   What have you done? Who did you meet?

            (*Pause.*)

JAMIE   Alright. Someone came round here yesterday
            afternoon for sex with me.

NIGEL   You what?

JAMIE   You heard me – someone came over for a shag.
         With me. They wanted to have sex with me.

NIGEL   (*laughing*) Who? Who would you get round here?

JAMIE   Who do you think? The first whore of
         anniversaries – your Cumboy17.

NIGEL   Why would he come round here? You haven't got
         a Gaydar profile.

JAMIE   I didn't need one. He came onto me when you
         went out to the shops yesterday morning. I kissed
         him, yes I did, and he tried to give me his number
         and told me to call him, said he wanted us to be
         fuck buddies, or boyfriends, he didn't know what
         he wanted.

NIGEL   You are joking!

JAMIE   But I didn't take the number. I didn't need to.
         When I got back yesterday afternoon he was
         standing outside the flat in the rain, staring up at
         the window. He was waiting for me, wanting *me*.

NIGEL   (*screams, exploding*) And you had sex with him
         while I was out? How could you.

JAMIE   I didn't. I turned him down!

NIGEL   You said you fucked him!

JAMIE   I said he came round here for sex – but he didn't
         get it. I sent him home.

NIGEL   Don't play with me Jamie!

JAMIE   He came onto me, he wanted me to go back with
         him to his, he wanted me to leave you and move in
         with him, it was insane, he said he wanted me to
         be his boyfriend. I was tempted for about two
         seconds just to see the look on your face – but I
         came to my senses.

NIGEL   Why? Why would you do that?

JAMIE   Because it felt wrong, because I was only doing it
             to get back at you and I was feeling sorry for
             myself, but he's a kid. Virtually a child. It's
             ridiculous. We spoke for a while – he was really
             upset. I got him some food and he stayed for that
             – and then I gave him a hug and sent him home in
             a cab. I said I would call him and maybe we would
             be friends with him, the both if us, but without the
             sex.

NIGEL   And you haven't spoken to him since?

JAMIE   No, of course I haven't.

NIGEL   I don't want you talking to him, I don't want to be
             friends with him after he did that. Where's his
             number? (NIGEL *searches*.) Has he got yours?

JAMIE   No.

NIGEL   Well good. I don't want to hear from or speak to
             or see him again.

JAMIE   Oh that's nice. He's had his use.

NIGEL   He's been more trouble than he's worth.

JAMIE   So now it's your turn.

NIGEL   I have been honest.

JAMIE   I will go.

NIGEL   This is fucked up. I'm telling you now, hand on my
             heart, on your life: the last person I had sex with
             was on Friday night with that little twat – Me, you
             and Cumboy.

JAMIE   Don't call him that!

NIGEL   Mark then! There's been no one else. I've been
             out with you, I went out with the boys to Orange
             last night, I missed you and I didn't even think
             about having sex with anyone. Not one person,
             not one time.

JAMIE   I just don't buy that.

NIGEL   It's the truth. And Friday night will be the last
             time ever if you say so. Until we split up. Or one
             of us dies. I love you, Jamie, why can't you
             understand that?

JAMIE   No, you don't. You're just with me because it's
             easy. You think 'Oh, good old Jamie, he'd never
             leave me, he's happy being second best', but I
             don't want to be second best any more. I don't
             want to be the runner up prize. I want someone to
             be with me because he wants to be with me.
             Because he loves me as much as I love him.

NIGEL   If you walk out that door then that will be that –
             you can fuck off onto the streets because this is
             my flat. Mine.

JAMIE   Even though I have paid for more of it than you
             have? We should sell it and split it down the
             middle.

NIGEL   Not legally. It's in my name – we can't get married
             remember – you can fuck off onto the streets for
             all I care. (*Pause.*) Cunt!

JAMIE   I knew you'd say something like that. That's
             exactly why I know I have to go.

             (JAMIE *picks up his suitcase and moves it to the
             door.*)

NIGEL   You can't leave me. You can't do this to us . . . for
             no reason.

JAMIE   It's for the best, Nige.

NIGEL   The best for who, eh?

JAMIE   If we do this properly now then maybe one day we
          can be friends.

NIGEL   But I don't want to be just friends.

JAMIE   Why not? We're barely that now.

NIGEL   How can you say that?

JAMIE   Do friends treat each other like this? Do we even
          like each other any more – we're never sober
          enough to find out. And just think – once we split
          up you can go and fuck whoever you want. At
          least I'll know you're telling me the truth. At least
          I will actually know where you are.

NIGEL   We can change.

JAMIE   You're just saying exactly what you think I want
          to hear. It's what you always do whenever
          anything like this happens.

NIGEL   No.

JAMIE   Will you just let me go? You have already hurt me
          SO much.

          (NIGEL *stand up and looks around panicked. He
          walks to the stereo, takes a CD out of the rack
          and puts it in the player.*)

          What are you doing? (*Pause.*) Nigel? (NIGEL
          *presses play and picks up the remote control. It is
          'their song'.*)

          Oh, turn it off . . . (*They stare at each other while
          the song plays.* NIGEL *points the remote control
          and turns it up as the verse kicks in.* JAMIE *bites
          his lip.*) Why are you doing this?

NIGEL   (*shouting over the music*) Because of ten years.
          Because . . . you're the only one I really want to

be with. (NIGEL *moves to* JAMIE *and puts his arm round him.* JAMIE *explodes and physically attacks* NIGEL *who restrains him without fighting back until* JAMIE *breaks down into a sob and into* NIGEL'S *arms. The following should be unrushed and give him time to cry.*) It's OK, it's OK. It's alright . . .

JAMIE   No, Nigel it's not. It's not going to be alright. It's not alright.

NIGEL   It's OK. Let it all out.

JAMIE   I love you so much.

NIGEL   I love you, too. Calm down . . .

         (*Pause.*)

JAMIE   Turn it down. You'll wake up upstairs.

NIGEL   I don't care.

JAMIE   Turn it down. (NIGEL *reaches over and grabs the remote and turns the stereo off. He hands* JAMIE *a tissue.*) I don't know what to do.

NIGEL   You don't have to do anything.

JAMIE   I can't go on like this.

NIGEL   We don't have to.

JAMIE   I don't want to go but we want different things. I want to calm down and that's just not you is it.

NIGEL   I want you. There's so much time between us, so much history. Are you going to throw that all away? Without expecting me to put up a fight. Come here baby.

         (*He holds* JAMIE, *then gets him another tissue.* JAMIE *wipes his eyes and blows his nose.*)

NIGEL   Leave me . . . don't be so silly. (*Pause.*) You know
            in this light you almost look ten years younger.

JAMIE   Do I?

NIGEL   You look like when we met. (*Pause.*) With us
            rowing.

JAMIE   We never did.

NIGEL   No, we didn't then did we? No, I mean it reminded
            me today . . . all these people blowing whistles in
            my ears for no reason whatsoever . . . pink turkey
            feathers flying round . . . You were looking at me
            as we were lining up to start the march.

JAMIE   And you're friend Anna the stripper came over
            and told me 'my friend fancies you'.

NIGEL   I can't believe she did that.

            (*Little pause.*)

JAMIE   You took advantage of my drunken state.

NIGEL   I did not!

JAMIE   Remember how difficult things were then, I was
            still at home, you could never come round.

NIGEL   Do you think people have it easier now.

JAMIE   I think so.

NIGEL   It was a nightmare when I was seventeen. No one
            to talk to. No one to turn to. That Mark's lucky –
            there's a million and one places you can go now.
            He can take people home as well.

JAMIE   I don't want to talk about him.

NIGEL   Me neither.

(*He squeezes* JAMIE. *Lights down on* NIGEL *and*
JAMIE. *Lights up on* MARK *as he enters and sits at*
NIGEL *and* JAMIE'S *PC.*)

Scene Two

Interior of MARK'S *bedroom, in front of his PC.*

MARK   Six messages, that's not bad is it? (*Little pause.*
            MARK *types something into the computer.*)

            I hate these early shifts. Especially the Sunday
            open. Bein' in when there's no one around. Except
            that fuckin' freak Martin. Duty manager. Always
            does the Sunday opens. Gets right on my tits.
            He's always sniffin' round me like a fuckin' dog. I
            told him, 'I'm straight, mate'. Makes me feel sick. I
            wouldn't go near him even if they did know. He
            still hangs round the whole time, like if he waits
            long enough I'm gonna go round the back with
            'im. As if. He's disgustin'. I've got ambition here.
            I wanna be a chef and maybe head chef one day so
            I gotta keep in with 'em. I ain't ever gonna get
            anywhere if they know about me. They say stuff to
            Martin, to his face, as if they like him, like they
            don't care that he's a queer but when he's not
            there they all lay into him. The other duty Tony
            warned me. He told me there's two queers who
            work here – Martin who's a dirty bastard and Neil
            who's just a wet little camp poof. He makes
            everyone laugh but they give all the shit jobs to
            'im. So I thought – better keep my gob shut. I
            know what people are like.

            (*Lights down on* MARK, *back up on* NIGEL *and*
            JAMIE.)

NIGEL   I really do wish my mum had been there on Friday.

JAMIE   You don't have to listen to what Lucy says you
            know. She's your mother, too. Maybe she's
            mellowed.

NIGEL   What, go through that again? Give her the chance
         to tell me to fuck off again. Great. I know I act like
         it's not a big deal – but it hurts me. It really hurts.

JAMIE   I know it does.

NIGEL   She wants me she can pick up the phone. I've got
         to have some dignity in this situation.

         (*Little pause.*)

JAMIE   You've got my mum and dad. You know they love
         you.

NIGEL   It's not the same though, is it.

         (*Lights go down on them, back up on* MARK.)

MARK   I said to my dad the day he threw me out. I said,
         'Where am I meant to go?' and he said, 'I don't
         fucking care, just get out of my house you dirty
         bastard'. Why would you say that to your own
         son? And I said that to 'im. I said, 'Dad, what do
         you mean? I love you, I'm still the same Mark, it
         don't matter, I ain't done nothin' wrong', but he
         slammed the door shut in my face. I didn't wanna
         cry, not in front of him or the neighbours and I
         didn't. I was really good. I was proud of myself. I
         held it in all the way out up the road. I ran to the
         154 stop and my lip was all quivering, like but I
         held it and I got on the bus and went all the way
         into Croydon without crying. I got off and I just
         had this feeling and I had to run down an alley. I
         cried so much I threw up.

         (*Lights down on* MARK, *up on* NIGEL *and* JAMIE.)

NIGEL   Ten years is a long time, isn't it? . . . Do you
         remember going to Palm Beach in Streatham?

JAMIE   Above the ice rink.

NIGEL   Yes. (*Laughs.*) The window which looked out over
        the rink where you could watch all the ice hockey
        players practising.

JAMIE   And they used to shout out 'Faggots!' and wiggle
        their arses at us.

        (NIGEL *laughs.*)

NIGEL   While we were standing there with out pink
        champagne cocktails. Dancing to Vogue. Twenty
        times a night. That was our first proper date.
        They'd just changed the age of consent to
        eighteen. You were legal, just. First time we
        danced together. First time we slept together as
        well.

JAMIE   We didn't sleep together on the first date?

NIGEL   No, we didn't. I was a gentleman. I can't believe
        you've forgotten that.

        (*Lights cross fade and rise on* MARK.)

MARK   I found this number for gays near here. Didn't
        think there were any but I called it and went to
        meet this bloke at East Croydon station. Dodgy
        looking twat in a knitted jumper, he was. He said
        we'd go back to his flat in his car to talk about the
        group. And we got there to this bedsit and he told
        me about everyone who goes and what they're like
        and what it's for. He sat me down and showed me
        a video of Gay Pride and gave me a copy of Boyz
        to welcome me into the gay world. Then he sucked
        my cock. He wouldn't fuck me though. I went there
        a few times but it was boring. And there was only
        one other sixteen year-old there. He wasn't my
        type. Not my kind of thing. Gaydar's easier. (*He
        looks at his PC screen.*) Still a lot of people on at
        this time in the morning. Shame I have to go to
        work. Complicatedmelody. What's that mean? He's
        fit, though. Maybe I could meet him in the week.
        Maybe I shouldn't meet anyone 'cos I'm a popular
        boy these days. (*There is a beep. He gets a*

message through.) This one's a dirty bastard.
Always messaging me. Won't take no for an
answer. 'Do you wanna come round here and give
me a blow job, mate?'. Well, it was no last month,
no last week and no today and it ain't gonna
change is it, you sad cunt. That's the best thing
about this. What you want. When you want it.
(*Beat. He clicks on his mouse.*) There you go.
Blocked.

(*Lights rise on* NIGEL *and* JAMIE.)

NIGEL   Lucky we met then. Lucky we had each other. I
          was quite lonely before.

JAMIE   You're not lonely now, are you?

NIGEL   How could I be? I could never feel lonely with
          you.

MARK   Was hoping Karen was gonna be in last night so I
          could show him off, say he wants to be me
          boyfriend. He's worth showing off. He's nice. Fit.
          Good body, good face, good cock, good job –
          nearly a hundred grand he's on, apparently.
          Getting a company car – Audi TT – in a month or
          two.

JAMIE   Everything was new back then. We were new. You
          only wanted me. Just you and me. I'd never been
          in love before.

MARK   Karen always says 'I make love, I don't have sex'.
          I always think that's shit, but I kind of think I
          know what she means now. It was amazing.

NIGEL   And I haven't been since.

          (*They kiss.*)

MARK   Sniffed coke off his cock at one point. That was
          cool. I said, 'course I've done it before'. But I
          hadn't. It was different from the way it normally is.

He was just . . . lookin' at me. I could feel it, it felt right . . . for both of us.

NIGEL   Come on then, let's go to bed.

JAMIE   I'll be in in a minute. I need to tidy up.

NIGEL   Leave it.

JAMIE   I can't leave it like this, it's a mess.

MARK   All the kids at school didn't want me, but he does. Shows what they knew. Fuck 'em.

NIGEL   I want to fuck you.

MARK   Fuck 'em all.

JAMIE   Do you now? I don't think I've got the energy.

MARK   From next week it's gonna be just me and him.

NIGEL   Do you want a glass of water? I'll get you one.

JAMIE   OK.

MARK   He's on line now. All the same, innit they. He'll have to come and get this later.

         (MARK *taps on his keyboard.*)

NIGEL   Oh Jamie, come here.

JAMIE   What?

MARK   He loves me. He told me.

NIGEL   I love you.

MARK   And I love him, too.

NIGEL   You know that, don't you?

MARK   I'd better get going.

JAMIE   Yes.

MARK   I know it.

JAMIE   Of course I do.

            (JAMIE *and* NIGEL *kiss twice methodically.*)

NIGEL   Where shall I drop you?

MARK   Wherever. Next train's not for ten minutes.

NIGEL   Come in for a cuddle.

JAMIE   Sounds nice.

MARK   You gonna give me your number then?

NIGEL   I don't think that's a good idea, do you?

JAMIE   In a minute. I just want to sit up and think.

NIGEL   I'll take yours. It'd be easier.

JAMIE   You go.

MARK   I hope you call.

NIGEL   Come to bed.

JAMIE   I will.

NIGEL   Course I will.

JAMIE   Five minutes.

            (MARK *clicks his mouse as the third noise we hear after their two kisses.*)

MARK   Sent.

            (MARK *puts on* NIGEL'S *coat.*)

NIGEL   Well don't stay up long.

JAMIE   Alright.

(NIGEL kisses JAMIE on the head and goes to bed. JAMIE goes and sits down on the sofa and sighs. After a moment we hear the noise of a message being received on Gaydar.)

JAMIE   Message. *(Pause.)* Nige, message.

(JAMIE gets up and goes to the bedroom and looks in. There is no answer. NIGEL is asleep. JAMIE walks over to the screen and clicks on it.)

JAMIE   'Message received at 6.58 am from Cumboy17'.

MARK   Hey Nigel, you horny bastard. Thanks for a great night. I've got your jacket here. Call me and you can come and get it today from work or you can pick it up when we talk about next week. Love, Mark. XXXXXXX.

JAMIE   Fuck you both.

(JAMIE gets up, breathing heavily. He paces round the room, not knowing what to do. He goes to the framed picture of the two of them on the bookcase and picks it up, slowly looks at it, back at the hallway to the bedroom. He puts it in his bag and goes to the door and puts his coat on. He looks and then gets up and goes to the computer and sits down at it and types and sends the message. MARK sits at his computer and we hear the noise of a message on Gaydar. MARK reads it.)

JAMIE   Hello Mark. This isn't Nigel, it's Jamie. Sorry if I've curdled your coffee. Hope you had fun with him again. I have. Lots of it. I know what you really want and I hope you get it with him but if you do want something more, then don't let any one tell you don't deserve it. Because you do. And so do I. *(Little pause.)* Good luck.

(*Little pause.* JAMIE *smiles and says warmly but ironically . . .*)

Gay. Pride!

(*Little pause.* JAMIE, *at the computer clicks the mouse. Once and then again and again.*)

Yes I am sure I want to log out.

(*He clicks again to log out. The computer goes off.* JAMIE *goes to the door, picks up his bag, opens the door and looks around the flat one last time. He leaves, shutting the door behind him. Blackout.*)